A **UDL** N

UDL

PLAYBOOK

for School and District Leaders

KATIE NOVAK AND MIKE WOODLOCK

Library of Congress Control Number: 2021909111

Paperback ISBN 978-1-930583-87-0
Ebook ISBN 978-1-930583-88-7

Published by:
CAST Professional Publishing
an imprint of CAST, Inc.
Wakefield, Massachusetts, USA

Bulk discounts available: For details, email *publishing@cast.org* or visit *www.castpublishing.org*.

Cover design by Lindie Johnson
Interior design and production by Happenstance Type-O-Rama

FROM KATIE

To Nani and Bapa.
I wouldn't be where
I am today without you.
And to Torin, Aylin, Brec, and Boden.
Be nice, work hard, and
lead with your hearts.
Love, Momma

FROM MIKE

To my wife and family who are
my reason for everything.
Thank you Keliann, Anna, Thomas, and
Kate for making my life amazing.

Contents

Introduction

Longtime college and university professor Reed Markham once said, "Successful leaders see the opportunities in every difficulty rather than the difficulty in every opportunity." It has always been true that as leaders, we have a choice of how we lead, inspire, communicate, and manage. This power and privilege doesn't go away in times of monumental upheaval. In many ways, global events of the past few years—the COVID-19 pandemic, conversations about racial justice, and widespread economic insecurity—have created opportunities to deconstruct our systems and build ones that are more inclusive, diverse, and equitable.

Traditional teaching just doesn't hold up when traditional structures are no longer in place. Thank goodness for that. We have an amazing opportunity at this juncture to unlearn some of the aspects of education that have been holding our learners, educators, families, and community members back for too long.

During the pandemic, educators and administrators who had committed to the principles of Universal Design for Learning (UDL) in earnest struggled far less with switching over to remote, hybrid, and concurrent learning landscapes. Why? They had flexibility in their repertoire. They did not rely on one tried-and-true method of delivery of content or assessment. Instead, they recognized barriers for what they were and considered how to pivot, ebb, flow, and change. Their commitment to iterative design helped them to adapt.

As administrators and leaders, we are faced with a mountain of difficulties, many of which have nothing to do with educating our students. We all know that hell hath no fury like a broken-down bus or a water leak in the boys' bathroom, and how those problems can derail our improvement efforts.

Still, this opportunity to rethink traditional education should not, and cannot, be ignored. Now, more than ever, educators all over the world need to fully commit to implementing UDL principles in their learning environments. As leaders in education, we have the power and the privilege to create a vision and strategy for this work.

Our current system, sadly, does exactly what it was designed to do—foster and exacerbate privilege. Although we have made great strides in the past few decades with increasing inclusion rates, implementing UDL and innovative practices in pockets, and adopting whole-school initiatives like restorative justice, we are *still* not meeting the needs of many of our students.

But that doesn't mean we can't.

Kurt Lewin theorized a model of change that is known as the *unfreeze-change-refreeze model* that requires prior learning to be rejected and replaced. Lewin asserted that human change is a process that involves painful unlearning without loss of identity and difficult relearning as one attempts to restructure thoughts, perceptions, feelings, and attitudes (Lewin, 1947).

Let's unpack that. Change is painful. It requires us to let go of beliefs we once had and start over. To make things even more complex, the process of change may attack our identity and make us question everything we thought we knew about ourselves as educators.

We love this concept of *painful unlearning* and its relationship to engagement. If we are to change, we have to unlearn the practices that have become second nature, even the ones we believe are working for most educators or for most kids. To do this, we have to admit to ourselves and others that something is wrong or imperfect, and when we do that, our ego takes a hit. As Edgar Henry Schein (1999), a former professor at the MIT Sloan School of Management, says, "Failing to meet our creative potential often looks more desirable than risking failure and loss of self-esteem in the learning process" (p. 60). But unfreezing involves just that. We have to recognize that our former belief systems are problematic, and we have to let go of them and replace them with a new model (the *refreeze*).

The book *Unlearning: Changing Your Beliefs and Classroom with UDL* (Posey & Novak, 2020) discussed the process of unlearning through the UDL lens. To motivate, engage, and empower learners, educators must not only learn about UDL but must first unlearn practices that don't work for all students. We, as school and district leaders, have to do the same. Even though it's painful.

We have all been there before, right? We are about to begin something that is going to change our lives for the better. We know if we start exercising today, and continue every day, we will be healthier and feel better in a couple of months. We know that if we break down and call a family member who we have been fighting with, we will be able to move past our anger and resentment and make upcoming gatherings more enjoyable. We know that if we want to make schools better for our students, we cannot keep doing the same things and hoping for the best. In many cases, we know these things intuitively but still find reasons to hold off. We put up counterforces, and then we stay exactly where we are.

Tackling a change as significant and large as changing the way education has been done for centuries is monumental in its scope. We have seen the next big thing come and go. This isn't just the next big thing. This is something different. UDL is a framework focused on designing better classrooms, better schools, and better districts. This framework is a reminder that variability exists and is a beautiful aspect of diversity, and it needs to be designed for.

Both of us love Paulo Coelho's (1998) book *The Alchemist*, especially as it relates to change in our lives. The story follows the tale of a shepherd boy, Santiago, as he leaves his home in search of the world's greatest treasure. In his travels, he meets the Alchemist, who shares wisdom that allows Santiago, and any reader, to find more purpose. Essentially, the book helps us to recognize that to find success, we have to follow what we know to be true in our hearts, even if there are barriers and obstacles along the way. The beauty of the journey, regardless of how challenging it may be, is that there are lessons to be learned with every misstep, every obstacle, and every struggle. May the same be true for your UDL journey.

We would not write this book if we were not 100% confident that building your leadership practice through the lens of UDL will make your schools better for your students, their families, and staff. Even if you are only able to implement some aspects of the framework at this time, it will still be beneficial.

So, to begin this book, we want to share a quote from *The Alchemist*, one to remind you about the importance of your journey and how what you wish for your school and district is the very thing that makes our work worth all the challenges that come our way: "It's the possibility of having a dream come true that makes life interesting."

1

Preparing to Be an Expert Learner

Like the burning sun rules the solar system, student learning and student engagement are at the heart of our schools and districts. They are the center of our work, around which every decision orbits. We serve so that all students have equal opportunities to succeed at high levels.

Or so we hope. If we are honest, as leaders, we likely spend too much time in meetings about meetings, making phone calls to vendors to negotiate prices on technology, and dealing with "buses, budgets, and BS." Add in student discipline, state reporting, and an avalanche of emails. And how about needing to answer difficult questions about social injustice? What about planning the logistics of in-person, hybrid, and remote scenarios, which can switch in an instant? Where did our focus on learning go?

Learning didn't go anywhere. It is still there among this avalanche of issues. And in many ways, we are so buried in these barriers that teaching and learning have taken a back seat. We have to fight to get back to where our attention, our talents, and our hearts need to be. In order to better manage all of the issues we face, school leaders all need to be expert learners.

In this work, from this point forward, you will be called to identify, and eliminate, barriers set in your path while also maintaining a strong core belief about student learning and how best to meet the needs of our kids, their families, teachers, and support staff in your buildings.

So, what does it mean to be an expert learner who is also a school leader?

In their book *Universal Design for Learning: Theory and Practice*, Meyer, Rose, and Gordon (2014) note: "An expert at learning is someone who is continually growing and developing through introspection and guided feedback from other experts and peers" (p. 26). They go on to provide reflection questions that help to optimize expert learning. We have adapted these questions to target instructional leadership practices. As we begin this journey together, take a moment and consider how you can consistently ask these questions in your practice as you think about your task of changing the outcomes of all learners despite the very real and very significant barriers that must be addressed.

Expert Learning Self-Reflection Questions for Leaders

- What are my strengths and weaknesses as a leader?
- What is the optimal setting in which I can learn to improve my practice?
- Which tools amplify my abilities and support my areas of weakness?
- How do I best learn from colleagues?
- How can I support myself when I feel anxious about an upcoming challenge?
- How can I be open to unlearning mistaken or outdated understandings and building new ones?
- How can I learn from my mistakes?

These questions highlight the importance of being reflective in your work. But as you reflect on your practice, the answers are not as simple as they seem. For example, take the question "What is your favorite place to vacation?" You may jump straight to answering "the beach," but then as you think more deeply, you may find yourself asking additional questions. What season is it? Who am I traveling with? If it's winter, you may find yourself dreaming of a slope-side ski chalet, instead, whereas summer may bring wishes for camping out under the stars.

Just like our travel plans, many of the questions to the reflective prompts may have different answers depending on the context, and that's okay. The reasons questions like this are ever-changing is because of a concept that will become critical in your UDL journey: *embracing variability.*

Variability recognizes that all learners (including you!) have a unique mix of strengths and weaknesses, and those are incredibly dynamic and depend on context. Our strengths and weaknesses are not static. In fact, they are ever-changing—and *changeable.* Understanding variability will help you as a leader recognize the power and promise of ongoing, consistent self-reflection.

Variability in an Open System

Effective leaders must reflect deeply and be open to change when faced with challenging situations because leadership is an open system. Open systems are not stable and they are ever-changing. To put this simply, you cannot adopt a leadership style and continue to ride that train to retirement. Too much in education changes (hello, COVID-19!), and we must be ready to make necessary adjustments so we can continue to lead in a changing system.

In the article "Critically Reflective Leadership: Defining Successful Growth," researchers Reardon, Fite, Boone, and Sullivan (2019) provide an analogy to explain an open system.

> Watch someone driving down a straight road. Ideally, no steering would be required. However, in even this most unchanging situation, the driver will make small adjustments to the steering. In a generic open system, feedback can be based on observed attributes of the context, inputs, processes, or outputs. Feedback is then used to adjust the system. Depending on the system and the situation, adjustments can be made to the inputs, the processes or even the contexts.
>
> For leadership, feedback is the process of critical reflection on the leader's style and practices. In other words, the critically reflective leader will be aware of personal goals, context, his or her own attributes and actions, and his or her impacts on the actions of individuals or the outcomes of organizations (p. 26).

Let's reflect on the statement "However, in even this most unchanging situation . . ." As leaders, we have to adapt even when our schools and districts are "unchanging," and goodness gracious, to say that education has changed in the past few years would be the understatement of the century. Think about the changes that are necessary in our own leadership in order to navigate the ever-changing new normal of our schools and districts.

Here is a list—admittedly, an incomplete one—of some of the predictable changes facing schools and districts in the wake of the COVID pandemic. In reviewing this very incomplete list, you can see why reflecting and asking for feedback is critical to help you and your team thrive. As you review our list, feel free to add your own bullets!

- ➲ Having the capacity to transition from in-person, to remote, to hybrid, and back again in a blink
- ➲ Leading and evaluating teachers from a distance (sometimes remotely!)

- Supporting educators to incorporate technology into both in-person and remote instruction

- Learning new technologies to continue to provide learning regardless of format

- Understanding and overseeing distancing measures, sanitation protocols

- Completing equity audits to identify disproportionality

- Creating strategic plans to ensure all students have access to multitiered systems of support

- Managing expectations of greater communication between home and school

- Managing expectations of multiple/varied forms of assessments and project-based learning despite one-size-fits-all standardized assessments

- Crosswalking multiple initiatives to support students, including UDL, Positive Behavioral Interventions and Supports, trauma-informed teaching, culturally responsive teaching, and antiracist practices

Once you see leadership as an open system, variability helps to explain why our own unique mix of strengths and weaknesses is incredibly volatile. The concept of variability is explored by Todd Rose (2016) in his book *The End of Average*. Rose, a Harvard lecturer, highlights three principles that make it clear that all of us must embrace variability in our schools, in our lives, and in ourselves.

The first is the *jaggedness principle* that makes it clear that everyone has a unique mix of strengths and weaknesses and, to make things more complicated, they change based on context. Every great leader has strengths and areas where they need to improve. When you consider your own leadership practice, you are likely aware of areas where you are confident, and other areas where you need support. In the book *Primal Leadership* (Goleman, Boyatzis, & McKee, 2013), the authors introduce the neuroanatomy of leadership and identify critical skills necessary to lead and inspire others and to drive change. The authors argue that very few leaders can be outstanding at all of these competencies, but an emotionally intelligent leader demonstrates mastery of at least half a dozen of them, preferably at least one from each domain.

Table 1.1 gives you an opportunity to reflect on your practice in terms of strengths and weaknesses. By plotting the attributes on the scale and drawing lines between them, you will notice jaggedness.

Table 1.1: Explore Your Jaggedness

	Low	Average	High
Self-Awareness			
★ Emotional self-awareness			
★ Accurate self-awareness			
★ Self-confidence			
Self-Management			
★ Emotional self-control			
★ Transparency			
★ Adaptability			
★ Achievement			
★ Initiative			
★ Optimism			

	Low	Average	High
Social Awareness			
★ Empathy			
★ Organizational awareness			
★ Service			
Relationship Management			
★ Inspirational leadership			
★ Influence			
★ Developing others			
★ Change catalyst			
★ Conflict management			
★ Building bonds			
★ Teamwork and collaboration			

The exercise in Table 1.1 can be misleading because, in fact, the results aren't always the same. The second principle outlined by Rose is the *context principle*, which means that context matters. When we think about our practice, we often think of strengths and weaknesses as being static, but that isn't at all the case in an open system. They can ebb and flow.

Let's say you have a reputation for being a reflective leader and you believe it's a relative strength. As a reflective leader, you may frequently survey your staff, students, and families about your leadership; facilitate dialogues to address staff culture; and advocate for restorative circles and justice over traditional discipline measures, not only with students but with staff. While being reflective may be a relative strength, this doesn't mean that you are always reflective. Remember that time you were tired? You had been up late at a school board meeting and then you received an email from a parent summing up all your flaws and lack of leadership in one neat email (ending with "regards," no less). Suddenly, you weren't so reflective. You were ticked off. You fired off a retort that was the exact opposite of reflective, and it felt pretty good to send that email. Now, why did such a reflective leader continue a virtual flame war? Because of the context principle.

The last principle is the *pathways principle*. It suggests that for any outcome you care about, there are multiple pathways to success. Given your own variability and the context of the moment, you need to be flexible! You have to be ready to reflect and then make adjustments, as the work is all about action.

We have both learned this countless times the hard way. In March 2020, we were given less than 24 hours to prepare for remote learning. Of course, we wanted to get it right. Although we are both committed to Universal Design for Learning (UDL), our first inclination was to create "expectations" for what remote learning would look like. As administrators, we tried to find the best answer to the questions "How long should students be online?" and "How much synchronous instruction should every student receive?" The context was so incredibly unknown that we fell back into the ole "tried-and-true practices" routines.

We don't really want to admit this, but for a moment, we thought the solution was to develop a clear and detailed method for delivering remote instruction to students, a template that all teachers could use to create lesson plans utilizing technology to the fullest. A reasonable approach to be sure. Identify problems and create a solution. Some of the problems included determining whether remote teaching would be synchronous or asynchronous, navigating a variety of different technological platforms and software, monitoring and supporting student social and emotional well-being, and addressing a severe lack of student engagement and motivation. There were more, but these were the headliners.

Several proposals were presented that provided specifics for all lesson plans that would address these issues. In our minds, every teacher in the building/district would use the template that would provide a uniform experience for students. The problem was that this was a 19th century solution to a 21st century problem.

Because we know that jaggedness exists among all of us, having a template that all teachers needed to follow seemed prescriptive and simplistic. After sharing the draft of our plan with educators in the district for feedback, we realized we needed numerous pathways for teachers to meet the needs of all learners. After those pathways were suggested, we shared them with students and parents for feedback. The firm goal was that all students would continue to learn, but we recognized there were numerous pathways.

We have been privy to too many amazing UDL lessons in our teachers' classrooms to allow a one-size-fits-all mentality to attempt to solve this problem. Why would we want to handcuff teachers who had embraced UDL over the last five years by telling them there was one way to meet the needs of their students? Ultimately it was determined that we would create an overarching list of "must haves" in our classes, or "firm goals," with flexible means. We identified that we needed to focus on the following items while planning lessons, and this was supported by staff, students, and families.

- Align all instruction to grade-level standards.
- Make sure to check in with all students daily.
- Utilize technology to effectively meet the needs of all students.
- Focus on student engagement and motivation.

When we think with a UDL lens, we must first identify what our goals are. Next, we utilized time to provide our teachers with the materials and information they would need to achieve the aforementioned goals. We provided professional development (PD) in a number of areas including UDL, technology opportunities, and social and emotional wellness.

As a result of this approach, we came away with a number of different ways in which to meet the needs of students and teachers during a very difficult time. Some teachers tackled remote and hybrid learning on their own while others employed a group mentality and worked in grade-level teams or departments. Teachers appreciated the flexibility in science classes to run some days asynchronously with remote students while they conducted labs with in-person students, while math teachers felt more comfortable teaching both remote and in-person students at the same time. Choosing a one-size-fits-all approach to addressing instruction and assessment during a pandemic may have been even less effective than doing so during a typical year.

Moving beyond a one-size-fits-all leadership style starts by recognizing our own jaggedness and taking steps to ask for feedback from others as to whether our own self-assessment is accurate. We recognize that students and staff both have significant variability, but as leaders, we also have strengths and weaknesses in our ability to make adaptive change, create a culture and a climate that values expert learning, and address a myriad of technical challenges like scheduling, budgeting, and meeting deadlines for evaluating staff.

Self-assessment alone isn't adequate to be a reflective, expert leader. In order to seek "guided feedback from other experts and peers," it's important to optimize mastery-oriented feedback from your staff.

Embracing Feedback as Professional Guidance

If we want to embrace what it means to be an expert learner, we need to encourage our colleagues and our learners to provide us with feedback, and both of us do that in frequent practice. Allowing staff to become mirrors of our instructional leadership is critical to foster self-reflection and continuous improvement, two hallmarks of expert learning. Now, this exercise is not for the faint of heart, but it's one that is absolutely critical to being an instructional leader because it helps to uncover professional blind spots.

Sara Canaday (2012), a career strategist and author of *You— According to Them: Uncovering the Blind Spots That Impact Your Reputation and Your Career*, writes about the importance of recognizing professional blind spots. She writes, "Otherwise talented people simply don't recognize that an underlying attitude or subtle behavior is hurting them and holding them back. Simply put, they just don't see the problem." Now, if you can't see a problem, you sure as heck can't solve it. And believe us, we know you may want to say, "But I *know* my strengths and weaknesses," but unfortunately that is what everyone says, and they are wrong. Experienced executive coaches reported in recent research that close to 90% of leaders lack self-awareness (Eurich, 2018). Even more disconcerting? One poll found that 90% of leaders believe that they are in the top 10% of performers.

So why do leaders have such weak self-perception? One theory is that when leaders, like us, reach higher-level positions, we are less likely to receive honest and direct feedback. We are often the evaluators, not the evaluated. That is why we have to seek out feedback, because it is what we most need to hear.

The Massachusetts Department of Elementary and Secondary Education (DESE) developed model feedback surveys to foster self-assessment in educators. The tool asks staff to anonymously rate their level of agreement with statements that address instructional leadership skills. Consider how your staff would respond if you asked them to reflect on your relative strengths or weaknesses in the following areas. Would they strongly agree? Agree? Disagree? Strongly disagree?

- ⮑ The principal/administrator suggests ways to keep students engaged in challenging lessons.
- ⮑ The principal/administrator supports staff to provide feedback on one another's practice.
- ⮑ When I receive training, the principal/administrator checks to ensure that the training made a difference and led to the intended outcome(s).
- ⮑ The principal/administrator encourages me to reflect on the effectiveness of my teaching practice.
- ⮑ If the principal/administrator identifies an area for improvement in my practice, there are effective supports in place to help me improve.
- ⮑ The principal/administrator seeks staff feedback to inform their own leadership practice.

When you reflect on this list of prompts, you may be thinking, "I would love to do all that, but I don't have the time." But here's the honest truth: You have to find the time for instructional leadership if you want to foster expert learning in your school or district. We are not in schools to manage; we are in schools to lead and inspire high quality, universally designed instruction in every classroom, for every learner, every day. And to do that, we have to embrace what it truly means to be a learner and model that for our staff.

One elementary principal provided staff with the complete survey tool and shared the following reflection about the process (Massachusetts Department of Education, 2016):

> *After receiving feedback from the staff about my performance, I took the areas my staff had suggested needed improvement and shared the results at a faculty meeting. Staff were given red, yellow, and green stickers and asked to rate how they saw*

> *me moving toward addressing the feedback they had given me.*
> *When the stickers were on the charts, the whole staff had an*
> *opportunity to look with me at my growth. The process mod-*
> *eled for the staff what it looked like to be transparent about*
> *practice, which helped me to move forward in my work to pro-*
> *mote a collaborative environment in the building; and it helped*
> *me monitor my own growth as a professional.*

If you are cringing thinking about the thought of publicly reflecting on feedback through the sticker exercise, take a deep breath and consider its power. When you, as a leader, share your areas of challenge and your plan for improvement, you are modeling what it means to be an expert learner, thereby minimizing the threat of acknowledging and addressing weaknesses throughout the school.

Now, we know there is no one-size-fits-all solution for asking for feedback. If the preceding example seems too daring for you, break up the process of feedback into smaller, manageable chunks. You can begin to seek out real and honest feedback for yourself in a myriad of ways without doing it on a huge stage. The following are potential next steps if you're not ready for a full survey.

- Begin by asking a trusted colleague for some real and honest feedback.

- Create an anonymous survey with a few reflection questions from those staff you evaluate or are in charge of leading in smaller groups.

- Take a page from leaders and those at the pinnacle of their respective fields and be willing to be a bit more vulnerable. It is difficult to do as we need to project confidence, but keep in mind that a strong culture is at the heart of a strong school. Folks that can balance being confident and in control with vulnerability often have more success in unifying others around a central idea. Take a look at Barack Obama, who was willing to join the Jimmy Kimmel show to read mean tweets about himself on national television. Kicking a staff meeting off with some mean tweet episodes is a great way to break the ice!

Now, quick caveat. Throughout this process, once your weaknesses, or areas of challenge, are identified, you don't want to go down a rabbit hole of self-pity. There will also be areas where you excel like crazy. You wouldn't be in a position of leadership if that were not true. Understanding weakness is important, but we can't forget about the areas where we have significant strengths and know that we can reach out to get the support we need to continue to grow. So, you want to make sure you embrace your full variability—not just the areas where you may need to focus improvement efforts.

The film *Apollo 13*, directed by Ron Howard and starring Tom Hanks, about the aborted moon landing in 1970, has been praised for its accuracy. One scene in the film reminded us of the importance of identifying the positives when addressing problems or barriers. During the planned moon landing, the astronauts faced a life-threatening situation when a small explosion crippled their vehicle. Understandably, both the astronauts and the engineers on the ground at NASA headquarters began to panic. After quickly assessing the myriad of things that were going wrong, chief flight director Gene Kranz silenced everyone and said, "Let's look at this from a standpoint of status. What do we have on the spacecraft that's good?" This changed the whole tenor of the command center. The engineers used Mr. Kranz's suggestion to facilitate an amazing effort to utilize what remained of the ship's systems to get the astronauts home safely.

As you begin to ask for feedback about your instructional leadership, you will identify areas where you need to focus your improvement efforts, but don't forget that your strengths will help to get you there. The same is true for your colleagues and all students. That is the magic of jaggedness and variability. Remember that an expert leader will continue to work toward a goal despite this jaggedness. Success is a game of overcoming weaknesses and failure and being vulnerable about the process.

The quality of our instructional leadership is directly related to fostering expert learning in our staff and through our staff to our students. We cannot reasonably expect people to follow a leader who lives by "Do as I say, not as I do." We must open ourselves up to a universally designed system that includes nontraditional leadership qualities like providing more choice for our teachers, and being more open, and more responsive, to their feedback and collaboration. This requires a certain vulnerability that may be difficult for leaders.

Brené Brown is the guru on vulnerability in leadership. In an essay, she states, "It's not fear that gets in the way of daring leadership. It's our armor." Brown (2018) goes on to say:

> What, if anything, about the way people are leading today needs to change in order for leaders to be successful in a complex, rapidly changing environment where we're faced with seemingly intractable challenges and an insatiable demand for innovation? There was one answer across interviews with 150 global C-level leaders: We need braver leaders and more courageous cultures.

Brave leaders acknowledge their weaknesses, seek feedback, foster collaborative culture, and distribute leadership to create adaptive change. And to create a courageous culture, a leader has to foster expert learning throughout the system. Only then do we have a chance of creating a universally designed system that meets the needs of all learners and challenges and supports all students, regardless of variability.

If you are willing to take this risk with your colleagues, they will be more likely to model this in turn to their colleagues and students. Once we have the strength and courage to admit where we need to improve, we are more likely to actually improve in those areas. This process of self-reflection is essential to leading a UDL-based school or district and essential to the UDL classroom. If it is not present at the leadership level, we should not expect to see it widespread throughout our learning environments.

Self-Reflection Questions for Leaders

1. What format of collecting feedback are you most comfortable with? Do you think it is important to go outside of your comfort zone when soliciting feedback? Why or why not?

2. How can feedback help you to better identify your perceived strengths and weaknesses?

3. What tools could you use to ensure that you are providing multiple options for your staff to give feedback in the way in which they are most comfortable?

2

The Executive Function of Leadership

n the movie *The Wizard of Oz*, Dorothy and Toto are going about their day when suddenly a tornado throws them into the magical Land of Oz. As administrators, we can relate. Countless times, we have sat down at our desks with a hot cup of coffee and looked at our schedule for the day. On our best days, we have blocked out time to work with small groups of students, visit teacher classrooms, and plan universally designed professional development for an upcoming faculty meeting. Ah, yes—all the important things. And then, the tornado comes in and wrecks a well-planned day.

Maybe it was the two days we spent investigating whoever kept making the equivalent of "poop snowmen" in the boys' urinals. Or maybe it was the time we ventured into the untamed jungle of middle-school girls' social media drama that spread into every classroom and hallway in the school. Or was it when our preschool student decided he didn't want to use the restroom and instead created his very own pee Slip N' Slide to enjoy in the back of the classroom? No school leader plans for these events, but when these tornados arrive, classroom observations and conversations about multiple means of representation get put on hold. Temporarily.

Then, when the tornadoes move on, we need the resolve to get back to the work that will effect positive change for our staff and students.

Universally designed leadership is about focusing on the larger goal to ensure that all students have equal opportunities to learn at high levels.

Executive Function and the
Four Disciplines of Execution

In the book *The 4 Disciplines of Execution* (2012), executive leadership coaches Chris McChesney, Sean Covey, and Jim Huling share a four-step process for driving change in an organization and building institutional executive function:

1. Focus on the Wildly Important

2. Act on the Lead Measures

3. Keep a Compelling Scoreboard

4. Create a Cadence of Accountability

Let's discuss these four disciplines through the lens of implementing UDL. First, it is critical that we focus on your *wildly important goals (WIGs)*. This principle asserts that while many of our goals are important, only one or two are *wildly* so. WIGs are the goals you must achieve, and research suggests that you can only focus on one or two of these at a time (McChesney, Covey, & Huling, 2012). In many schools and districts, the wildly important goal is clear. We are called to eliminate inequities among learners.

The challenge, of course, is staying focused in spite of the tornadoes. We always have a tendency to add more to our plate, to extend our reach, and in doing this, we are our own worst enemy. If we are not focused, we are not effective. Of course, the pee Slip N' Slide needs to be cleaned up, right? But doing so doesn't exactly advance the critical work of giving students equal opportunities to succeed at high levels, providing access to advanced coursework, and offering authentic assessments. So how can we create long-term strategies that drive improvement efforts while still taking care of everyday business?

That's where the second discipline comes in. We need to apply "disproportionate energy" to the activities that drive our lead measures (p. 44). Wait, lead measures? McChesney, Covey, and Huling distinguish between lead measures and lag measures. *Lag measures* represent the ultimate outcome you want to see, something like a summative assessment. *Lead measures* concern the activities that, well, *lead* to that outcome. They are the things most connected to achieving your WIGs. Lead measures are the formative steps and assessments you make to ensure that you are staying on the path toward your final objective. They are the things you can do now—activities you control—to work toward your ultimate goal. For example, here is a sample of evidence-based targets—or lead measures—that will help you to work toward eliminating inequities.

- ❍ Facilitate an educator evaluation process to provide formal and informal feedback related to meeting the academic, behavioral, and social-emotional needs of all students in inclusive settings to improve practice and impact student achievement.

- ❍ Work to create a schedule that allows time for evidence-based instruction and interventions to be delivered across all three tiers in order to meet the academic, behavioral, and social-emotional needs of students.

- ❍ Ensure all staff have a firm understanding of the components and value of inclusion and inclusive practice and believe that all students can be successful with appropriate levels of support.

◐ Ensure adequate professional development to support the foundations of inclusion (such as PD on UDL and culturally sustaining practices) that are embedded into the district and school PD plans.

◐ Identify fidelity measures to assess the implementation of evidence-based strategies, instruction, and interventions. Create clear processes to determine how, when, and who will assess the fidelity measures.

Let's take a single target from this list—"Facilitate an educator evaluation process to provide formal and informal feedback related to meeting the academic, behavioral, and social-emotional needs of all students in inclusive settings to improve practice and impact student achievement"—to show the difference between lag measures and lead measures.

We can all agree on the importance of staff feedback. As an evaluator, it is critical that you elevate and celebrate the voices of the educators you evaluate. Imagine sending out an anonymous survey to educators in which you ask them to choose their level of agreement with the following statement:

My evaluator provides me with informal and formal feedback that helps me to improve my practice and impact student achievement.

You ask educators to rate their level of agreement from strongly agree, agree, and disagree to strongly disagree. When you get the results, you are looking at lag measures. Essentially, the data shares an evaluation of *what has already occurred.* You can't go back and change the past, but you can definitely set daily or weekly goals that will "lead" you to better outcomes. The lag measures may get you down, but you have to translate them into action. If you want more educators to perceive your feedback as relevant, authentic, and meaningful, you may have to do things differently.

In this scenario, you may decide that you need to carve out three hours a week to observe classrooms informally (whether in person or virtually) and write up mastery-oriented feedback aligned to evidence-based strategies and inclusive practices. You may also want to reach out to each educator to ask them their preferred way of receiving informal feedback. Consider an email like the following:

> Thank you so much for taking the time to complete the survey about evaluation feedback. As administrators, we take your feedback to heart. Many of you do not yet find that the feedback we provide is helping you increase the outcomes of all students, so we are going to do better. We have set a lead measure for ourselves to spend at least three hours a week in classrooms to offer informal feedback aligned to research on eliminating inequities. We would love for you to choose how you'd like to receive this feedback. We can share via email, via text, or face to face (in person or on Zoom). Next month, we will share the survey again and hope to see our own growth.

Your lead measure is something that can be done now, can be measured, and is predictive. If you commit to observation, take time to align feedback to high-yield strategies, and deliver in ways that meet teachers' needs, you will likely see improvement the next time you give the survey. Together, lead measures and lag measures help you monitor your progress toward your targets as you keep your wildly important goal in mind.

Note how this scenario weaves in the power of expert learning, feedback, and executive function as you model what it means to focus on the wildly important. Now, we are fully aware that committing to three hours per week will be difficult, given all the emergencies that pop up from day to day, but the investment in action that will help move your educators forward is critical to eliminate inequities among learners.

The third discipline is that of true engagement. For this, you need to keep a compelling scoreboard. In short, you need to have a visual reminder that allows you to continue to work toward your

WIGs despite the whirlwind of to-dos that come your way. To be accountable to your lead measures, you need to keep track of them. *True engagement* depends on attention and commitment, and on sustaining effort and persistence as you work toward your goals. If you don't keep track, if it's not front and center, you will find it difficult to determine if you have met your targets.

The last discipline is to create a *cadence of accountability*. Share your scoreboard and your results with your team. Great teams operate with a high level of accountability, so it is critical that your team is on the same page about your goals, targets, and scoreboards. If you don't share these, no one will know if you are committed. Meet with your team weekly and share your progress so you can publicly learn from successes and failures and also make new commitments for the following week.

We know this may seem like a lot, but without this commitment, we know well that true progress won't occur. The four disciplines of execution are a great tool to help you set goals, monitor progress, and work toward the accountability of your team behind you. Making this commitment is essential if you are to make adaptive change in your organization.

In the next section, we will discuss two types of leadership: technical and adaptive. Both of these are necessary for improvement, but adaptive leadership is the real work that requires collaboration, creativity, and innovation. Technical solutions in our schools are absolutely necessary but not sufficient if we are going to achieve our wildly important goals.

Technical vs. Adaptive Leadership

Back in the 1980s, Nintendo was all the rage. One of our favorite games, Super Mario Bros., provides a solid analogy for being an educational leader. Not only do we have to acknowledge our own strengths and weaknesses, but we also have to foster collective growth toward a goal, despite the barriers in the system.

In Super Mario, the goal was to get to the castle, but those darn turtles, "Koopa Troopas," and "Goombas" were always getting in the way. We got such great satisfaction from squashing those buggers so we could focus on the castle. Leadership is a little like that.

As we shared previously, we do not have to search far and wide to identify the barriers that take away from what is the most important part of being an instructional leader in a school or district. Reaching our goal of success means eliminating, or squashing, what is preventing us from getting there. But some barriers are much easier to address than others, and having a solid understanding of the two types of barriers will help you to set goals and strategies for eliminating them.

There are two different types of barriers: The pesky Koopa Troopas who pop up unexpectedly throughout the day and the more systemic barriers—the gatekeepers that result in institutional inequality and ineffectiveness—like that evil Bowser who lies waiting under the surface.

Heifetz and Linsky (2002) identify two types of challenges when instituting change, adaptive and technical, in the aptly named book *Leadership on the Line: Staying Alive Through the Dangers of Leading.* They define technical challenges as short-term problems that can be solved by the knowledge of experts, whereas adaptive challenges, which require new learning, result in long-term outcomes, and require collaboration with multiple stakeholders.

Take a look at the examples in Table 2.1. The barriers in the first column are examples of the technical aspects of leadership, whereas the long-term barriers require strategic thinking and adaptive solutions.

Table 2.1: Technical and Adaptive Barriers

Technical Barriers	Adaptive Barriers
★ Phone calls from parents	★ Lack of support from district office
★ Student discipline	★ Insufficient professional develop-
★ Utilities issues	ment to enact change
★ Bus problems	★ Poor culture
★ Teacher coverage	★ Fear of failure
★ Reporting requirements	★ Lack of funding

When the problem and procedure for addressing barriers are clear, you are dealing with a technical change. For example, when a parent calls because a child didn't get off the bus, you know what you need to do. You get on the phone, call the bus company, track down the student. It's clearly important work, but it's the kind where the steps that you take are laid out. You've been there, done that. When students get sent to the office for bullying or vaping, there are procedures and protocols in place to address the students.

But bigger issues lurk beneath the surface that require long-term commitment, continuous improvement, and change. Or, as we like to say—expert learning and leading. Simply addressing technical barriers does not allow us to transform our schools and provide all students with equitable opportunities to succeed. Transformation requires us to address much more systemic barriers, or adaptive problems.

If you have a negative staff culture, you can't just pick up the phone and fix it. You can't read a blog online or show a video and solve it. No procedures address what to do when your staff feels hopeless, not listened to, and uninspired. Sure, you can host a morning coffee as a technical Band-Aid, but that won't solve your problem. Adaptive challenges require tenacity. You have to collectively create a vision, distribute leadership, identify the barriers head on, and create strategic plans to fulfill that vision using the four disciplines of execution. The follow-through of implementation may take years. This is the work we are called to do.

In his military days, Dwight D. Eisenhower once said, "Plans are useless but planning is indispensable." There is great wisdom in this statement. The job and the daily, often unexpected, technical demands take away from our priorities, and they may impact our short-term plans, but staying true to our wildly important goals is a part of what makes us strong instructional leaders. When we veer off course, we have to recognize the barriers, eliminate or delegate them, and then refocus on our goals. We cannot reasonably expect others to engage in this endeavor if we do not prioritize it and our role in the process.

When the COVID tornado blew apart the 2019–2020 school year, we faced significant barriers that forced us to concentrate much more heavily on many of our technical barriers as well as adaptive barriers that were not even on our radar a month earlier. Eliminating inequities in a virtual space required a significant shift in strategies and tactics.

Gradually, though, we found ourselves digging out of the rubble and making small yet important strides toward our wildly important goals. Our best advice in such times: Be fair to yourselves and understand that you may need to take one step forward and two steps back. But do not take your eyes off of your main goals and your lead measures. Model grit and perseverance for your staff while doing your best to recognize the difficulties that they are all going through. When you feel stuck, ask for their feedback.

Adaptive challenges and expert learning require you to foster collaboration and community. To address adaptive challenges, you need a team, one that includes all of your colleagues, who can assist, provide feedback, offer solutions, and monitor progress. As a leader you are likely to be the point person. This is expected. That does not mean that you should be losing sleep at night attempting to identify solutions to all of the struggles that go along with being an instructional leader. You will hear this echoed throughout the pages of this book: "You need a team." Onboarding and coaching willing and competent team members whom you can lean on when your time is compromised is a key to the success of UDL implementation on a large and effective scale and a critical aspect of instructional leadership and adaptive change.

Just like we preach to our staff and students, we need to be resilient, be flexible, and persevere, even when things do not go according to plan. And we also have to be open to feedback. Ask your staff, "Does anyone have any advice on how I can better schedule my time and commitments so I can work more closely with you all on the most important aspects of our work?"

While we may spend a lot of time analyzing what needs improvement in our schools, we can't forget that at our core, we are learners, and we are both a part of the problem and a part of the adaptive solution if we embrace expert learning.

Self-Reflection Questions for Leaders

1. How can you make your wildly important goals so clear that daily obstacles and moments of pure absurdity cannot alter your direction significantly?

2. As you consider your learning environments, what are the technical and adaptive barriers that you are currently focused on addressing through your leadership?

3. How will creating feedback loops help you stick to your leadership goals? Read the following case study and reflect on/discuss how you would handle the situation given what you know about technical and adaptive leadership.

─────────── Case Study Discussion ───────────

Imagine you consistently observe a teacher who is committed and passionate but who struggles significantly with content and classroom management. Students in this teacher's class have come to you with concerns, and you have met with the teacher numerous times. You have faith that this teacher will improve, but you want to put her on a short-term improvement plan to increase accountability and support growth.

Fifteen minutes before the meeting where you will share this with her, you receive a report of a loss of water pressure. The toilets aren't flushing. You don't have an assistant principal and your secretary is out. Clearly, you know that your meeting with the teacher is critical and required for her professional improvement, but public health requires your attention. How many times are we in similar situations? They are crappy (pun intended)!

Addressing water pressure issues requires a technical solution, but improving the efficacy of your teaching staff is an adaptive solution that will need to be addressed through goal-setting, ongoing coaching and professional development, numerous observations and feedback, and collaborative culture. Take a moment and reflect on this situation. If you're with colleagues, address how you would handle this situation, balancing both the importance of technical and adaptive challenges and expert learning.

3

Creating a
UDL Foundation

The *broken windows theory* in criminology states that visible
signs of lawbreaking create an environment that encourages further crime. In *The Tipping Point*, Malcolm Gladwell
(2000) cites extensive research that illustrates that the broken
window theory explains how subtle, minute, and often uncon-
scious influences can affect human behavior. Likewise, creating
a culture of inclusion and diversity requires a school culture that
fosters it. UDL reminds us to eliminate barriers that prevent
schools from building conditions of nurture and to facilitate a culture that supports expert learning.

We have discussed that developing a culture of expert learning needs to start with you as a leader. If we want to create environments in which educators can grow and change, we have to
be willing to model this ourselves. As a school leader, once you've
figured out how to prepare for expert learning and be open to
formative feedback, it is time to engage your teachers/staff in
doing the same. To do this, you have to work hard to create conditions of nurture where staff can be vulnerable, take risks, and
grow. To do this, you have to focus on instructional leadership,

relationships, and understanding that UDL is a framework that requires you to shift your beliefs and invest your time and energy differently.

In a recent study, teachers were interviewed about the barriers that prevented them from implementing UDL (Scott, 2018). One of the biggest barriers cited was a lack of administrative support. Zoom back and consider how devastating this is. It would be like asking students why they aren't learning and they answer, "Lack of teacher support." Yikes. So, before you can make adaptive change, you have to create a culture that embraces change. To do that, you need to understand the core components of UDL and how it creates a framework for a multitiered system that meets the needs of all learners, educators, and families.

UDL as a Framework

To create a universally designed system, it's critical that you are able to articulate the core values that shape the UDL framework and model them within your practice. Often, educators hear about UDL and think of it as a list of strategies or a checklist, and that won't result in the adaptive change that is necessary to create a more inclusive, equitable system. UDL isn't a set of prescribed actions—the UDL principles may suggest very different actions in different contexts. There is, however, at UDL's foundation, a set of fact-based beliefs and values drawn from the learning sciences and evidence-based practices. Once you align to the core values of UDL, strategies continue to evolve and are flexible and iterative based on students' voices and needs.

What are those fact-based UDL values and beliefs? A UDL practitioner knows this:

- ◗ Variability is the rule, not the exception. Learners may need to learn in different ways, using different materials, to reach the same goals.

◐ All students can work toward the same firm goals and grade-level standards when provided with conditions of nurture and adequate support.

◐ All learners can become expert learners if barriers are removed.

These truths are the seeds of UDL. All the UDL Guidelines in the world won't transform practice if they aren't in service of the belief that all students can learn. Your culture begins to shift when you recognize the value of variability, equity, and inclusion. To get there, you need to design for it. This is where the UDL principles come into play: Provide multiple means of engagement, multiple means of representation, and multiple means of action and expression (Rose & Meyer, 2002). We will now explain each of the principles further.

Provide multiple means of engagement. Engagement is at the core of all learning experiences. If we want to empower our learners, we have to foster both attention and commitment by designing flexible, authentic, and meaningful experiences for them to learn.

On the surface, engagement is often thought of as students who are involved in the classroom and are able to actively participate, but the research suggests that engagement is far more complex. Engagement is equal parts attention and commitment (Schlechty, 2011). Commitment requires both the ability to sustain effort and persistence and the ability to self-regulate and cope with the rigor of academics and the classroom environment. Students are not the only ones who are impacted by a lack of coping skills. Researchers argue that teachers' ability to cope affects students, as those teachers who are socially and emotionally competent are more likely to create a classroom environment that explicitly teaches important self-regulation skills to students so they can be more successful with their learning (Iizuka et al., 2015).

Provide multiple means of representation. The second principle of UDL reminds educators to provide multiple means of
representation to build knowledge and comprehension in all
learners. Not all learners comprehend information in the same
way, have the same background information, or have access
to the same vocabulary. We must provide multiple access and
entry points so all students can grow as learners as they reach
toward the same goal.

When teachers present information, they often use a single
representation and provide the same lesson to all students.
This may be done in a lecture, by playing a video, or by presenting or demonstrating information, teaching vocabulary, and so
forth. Because learners vary significantly, the information they
need to gather to perform an authentic assessment will vary
as well. When we provide multiple opportunities and options
from which students can learn information, these learners are
empowered to personalize how they build knowledge and skills.

Provide multiple means of action and expression. Learners
need to not only comprehend information but also express
what they know and demonstrate what they can do. Learners benefit from having numerous methods for showing their
understanding as they develop into writers and speakers in
ways that are developmentally appropriate for them and that
embrace emerging technologies.

Traditionally, students were asked to share their understanding using only one means of expression. When teachers provide
them with multiple options, learners are able to practice executive functioning skills as they analyze the task and choose the best
option to demonstrate that they have met the intended outcome.

Essentially, the principles drive design by rooting the design of
teaching and learning with three core questions:

- What is it that all learners need to know or be able to do?

- Based on variability, what barriers may prevent students from learning?

- How do I design flexible pathways for all learners to learn and share what they know?

This framework will become the foundation for your leadership practice and how you work to create the beliefs, skills, and system that are necessary to ensure all students have equal opportunities to learn.

Australian education researcher Charles Kivunja (2018) writes about the struggles many graduate students have distinguishing between theory, theoretical frameworks, and conceptual frameworks. The distinctions outlined by Kivunja are helpful for thinking about how UDL helps to create an environment that allows all stakeholders to thrive in your school or district:

- A *theory*, emerging from a long process of research, is a logical and coherent set of principles intended to explain some phenomena. The theory underlying UDL is made up of those beliefs and values we discussed earlier.

- A *theoretical framework*, he writes, is a synthesis of the thoughts of experts in your field and how you use those theories to understand your practice. UDL—and the accompanying Guidelines—forms a theoretical framework that informs your practices.

- A *conceptual framework*, writes Kivunja, "is the total, logical orientation . . . of anything and everything that forms the underlying thinking, structures, plans and practices and implementation" of a particular research initiative. In other words, a conceptual framework, which informs your learning process as a UDL practitioner, is metacognitive, reflective, and operational, and thus, it requires you to be an expert learner.

To explain the relationship between a theoretical framework and a conceptual framework, Kivunja compares the conceptual framework to a house and the theoretical framework to a room that serves a particular purpose in that house.

Drawing on Kivunja and the four disciplines of execution discussed in the previous chapter, the following questions can help guide the development of your conceptual framework:

1. What do you want to accomplish in your practice?

2. Why do you want to do it?

3. How do you plan to do it? For example, which action steps, or lead measures, will you take to effect change?

4. What "data" will you collect to reflect on and inform your practice?

5. How will you share your findings with relevant stakeholders to create a cadence of accountability?

Embodying Core Values

If you are going to lead everyone in a new direction, they have to know where they are going. When a school is committed to implementing Universal Design as a conceptual framework, the core principles of the framework need to inform the development of a vision statement, a mission statement, core values, or, in the case of a high school, the vision of a graduate to guide the long-term work necessary for adaptive change.

Regardless of the format, *core values*, as we will call them, need to be more than just something that you can find on a poster in a classroom or headlining the school website. Core values undergird everything we believe to be true about teaching and learning and serve as the foundation of our school culture. Core values often include a shared desire for all children to feel safe, welcome, respected, heard, affirmed, supported, and valued in school (Haslam, 2018).

When considering the core beliefs of the UDL framework, we are struck by core values that UDL practitioners need to embody. If we want to foster expert learning and build deep engagement, we need to articulate our beliefs in core values that impact our school culture. We see the following core values as explicitly connected to the UDL framework.

- Community
- Engagement
- Equity
- Flexibility
- Inclusion
- Perseverance
- Relevance
- Respect
- An unwavering belief in all students' potential

In the following section, we will discuss how these core values support educators in creating a universally designed system that is proactive, flexible, and iterative.

Pause and Think

Now that you have learned more about the importance of being an expert learner and the power and promise of adaptive change, what core values would you love to embed in your school community? Take a moment and add to our list. What values are necessary to create a system that is universally designed?

If we want to create a system that is focused on UDL, our core values need to align to the core beliefs of the framework. It is critical to do this work collaboratively with all stakeholders to ensure there is shared responsibility for the core values.

The following questions are great prompts to ask your staff to help begin this conversation about core values.

- Which of our core values is our school community in need of the most?
- How will we embody these core values through our practice?
- How will we recognize these core values when we see them in our classrooms?

You can ask the same questions of students and families. Once you have articulated core values with your school community, you have an important lens through which you can begin to assess your practices and procedures. Take perseverance, for instance. We all want learners to not give up, to push forward even when things get difficult, but are we creating a culture of perseverance with our staff and students? Let's start with our staff.

- Do we offer opportunities for collaboration and community, co-planning, and mastery-oriented feedback?
- Do we encourage risk-taking and trying new things, taking the chance that doing so may affect student outcomes in the short term?
- Do we create options for self-regulation so our colleagues can cope with the frustration and challenge that comes with perseverance?

If the answer is no to any of these questions, we will not have true engagement with staff, and we won't see the core value trickle down to learners.

Core values not only contribute to improving school culture; they also shift the culture in ways that matter to learning (Redding, Corbett, & Center on School Turnaround at WestEd, 2018).

We must make the core values known to everyone who is invested in the success of the school and its students. This will help create community and common purpose. It is especially important that school leaders embrace core values and use them as a compass to guide decision-making. Research shows that school principals are required to make value-based judgments in more than half of administrative decisions, and those decisions can often become clearer and more intentional when they filter issues through core values (Larsen & Hunter, 2014).

We should also note that understanding the UDL framework and articulating core values is necessary but not sufficient to begin the UDL journey. UDL creates a foundation for Tier 1 instruction that values equity and inclusion, but we would be remiss not to mention that some students may need additional support to grow as learners. All students deserve access to universally designed instruction with their peers, but as practitioners, we are sure you recognize that some learners may need more support than that. This is where a multitiered system of support (MTSS) comes in. Helping staff understand how UDL creates a foundation for a multitiered system is important for the critical work that comes next.

UDL to Create Multitiered Systems of Support

To meet the needs of all learners, we have to create inclusive and equitable systems that ensure that all students have equal opportunities, access, and expectations to learn at high levels. We need to make sure they are getting the support they need in academic, behavioral, and social-emotional development in order to succeed. We need to ensure that educators have the tools they need to accomplish these goals. To do this, we have to challenge beliefs, skills, and our systems so our work is learner-driven and evidence-informed. To do this, we need to create a multitiered system of support (MTSS). We would like to share an analogy to help you better understand how UDL creates the foundation for this system.

Both of us drive SUVs. They are perfect cars when you have kids who lug around giant lacrosse and hockey bags and you need to tow around the family dog. Now, we have very firm goals for our cars: We need them to run smoothly and safely. So, we always make sure that we get our routine services.

Tier 1 at the mechanic involves an oil change, topping off of fluids, a tire rotation, and a good vacuuming. We expect to get these services regardless of the make and model of our car. During this Tier 1 onceover, the mechanic uses numerous universal screening measures to determine if our SUV needs additional services. They check all the engine fluids, the tire pressure, and the windshield wipers; they hook up machines that talk to the engine to see if there are any potential problems. Sometimes, as a result of this screening, we need more services. The oil change appointment might quickly morph into a radiator, muffler, or tire replacement appointment. These are second level (Tier 2) services that we only need to get when those fancy assessment machines and mechanics tell us we need them.

What is important to note is that when Tier 2 services are necessary, we don't lose out on Tier 1. The mechanic doesn't say, "Sorry, but since you need your transmission serviced, you can't get the oil changed." Why? Because that would lead to more problems. In many cases, the same mechanic can perform both Tier 1 and Tier 2 services right at the same place and time. And we don't have to get those Tier 2 services every time just because we needed them now. Once the mechanics have shown that the additional services have done what they need to do, we are free to go back to just getting the oil change.

But let's say the problems continue even after the transmission service. The car is jolting about when we get on the highway and makes a funny noise. We take the car in for a Tier 2 service again, but maybe that isn't enough. Maybe the car needs more support. Let's say we need a whole new transmission. Again, that doesn't mean we can't get our oil changed! This procedure might be classified as a level three service (Tier 3), and even fewer people need these services, but when you need them, we guarantee you will be thrilled they are available. As the level of service goes up, the repair is more intensive and progress monitoring is critical. Sometimes, the level three service might be out of the mechanic's wheelhouse (see what we did there?!), and you'll need to bring your car elsewhere. Others may be able to handle it just fine.

Are you still with us? Essentially, when your car needs services, you should be able to get those services. And the same is true in our schools. When we have a comprehensive system of support, our schools offer multiple levels of support to students, when they need it. Higher levels of service don't replace the need for maintenance services. It's about supplementing, not supplanting, those services.

UDL is critical to ensure that Tier 1 meets the needs of all learners so that everyone can be educated in the least restrictive environment available. Multitiered support systems are recommended in the Every Student Succeeds Act (ESSA) as a "comprehensive continuum of evidence-based, systemic practices to support a rapid response to students' needs, with regular observation to facilitate data-based instructional decision making."

Figure 3.1 provides a representation of an MTSS model that is proactively built from the outside in. All learners receive Tier 1, where they have opportunities to access grade-level rigor and behavioral and social-emotional support. For this to work, we need to build the skill level of educators and the vision of leadership and have the necessary tools to support students (that is, the drivers).

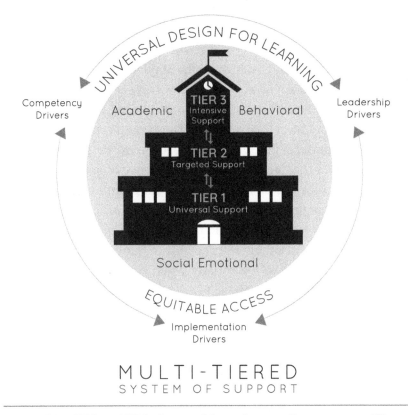

MULTI-TIERED
SYSTEM OF SUPPORT

Figure 3.1: MTSS and UDL. Source: Massachusetts Department of Elementary and Secondary Education, 2019, p. 5.

If we zoom back to the mechanic analogy, an auto shop needs skilled mechanics who can work with multiple makes and models and who have numerous tools to diagnose issues and address them immediately. They also need fluids, tools, and an auto lift. We can't expect mechanics to fix our cars if they don't have the right tools. And lastly, who are the leaders who are committed to ensuring high-quality customer satisfaction, ongoing communication, and a vision for success? How much more difficult would it be to get our cars fixed if say, the hours of operation were only 2 to 5 a.m.? That system doesn't support improvement for many.

Tier 1 is universal support. It is the foundation of the system and is equitable and all-inclusive. All students will receive Tier 1 support as they walk into the front door of the school as the visual in Figure 3.1 suggests. Students will receive more support as necessary for their individual needs when data suggests it is necessary.

Tier 2 builds on Tier 1 rather than replacing it. Tier 2 services may or may not supplement special education services for students with an individualized education plan (IEP), depending on the individual student's needs. The arrows to Tiers 2 and 3 represent "elevators," and students may move up and down the tiers as data suggests they would benefit from more targeted and intensive support. For example, a student with an IEP for reading comprehension may receive Tier 2 targeted supports for math. Another student with an IEP might receive Tier 3 intensive supports for behavior and Tier 1 universal supports for academics.

Tier 3 is for intensive support that often includes explicit, skills-based, focused interventions that occur individually or in very small groups. Again, Tier 3 supports are provided for all students who need them. Tier 3 is not synonymous with special education. Students who receive Tier 3 supports may remain in the same physical location as students only receiving Tier 1 or Tier 2 or both supports.

If we can provide the services we need for our cars, we sure as heck can create systems that provide those supports, when they are needed, for our kids. Certainly, we could share a lot more about MTSS, but the focus of this book is on creating inclusive, equitable classrooms and cultures that welcome, engage, and support all learners through the principles of UDL. To learn more about multitiered systems of support, we recommend reading the Massachusetts Department of Elementary and Secondary Education's "Multi-tiered System of Support: A Blueprint for MA." See https://matoolsforschools.com/resources/mtss-blueprint to download the report. Katie Novak and Kristan Rodriguez, coauthors of *Universally Designed Leadership* (CAST, 2016), also coauthored the Massachusetts blueprint.

Self-Reflection Questions for Leaders

1. Why is it critical to understand UDL as a conceptual framework as opposed to a list of strategies?

2. Do I truly believe in the power of variability, that all students can access grade-level rigor, and that all students can become expert learners? If not, how can I expect my staff to align their practices to the framework?

3. As a school, do we have core values? If so, do they align to the core principles of UDL? If not, how can we begin the process of revising them?

4. Recognizing that UDL provides a foundation for a multi-tiered system, how can I ensure that all students in our system get what they need, when they need it, while also having opportunities to become expert learners?

4

Modeling UDL Through Professional Learning

lanis Morissette penned the song "Ironic." Not to date ourselves, but when we were in high school, we rocked out to that song. If we could go back in time, we would tell Alanis to add a line about UDL professional development (PD). It would go something like this, "It's the sit-and-get of UDL PD. Who would have thought? It figuuuuures." (It's catchy, isn't it?)

The UDL framework creates a rigorous and nurturing environment for all learners because it focuses on providing all of them with options so they can take ownership of their learning; become motivated, self-directed problem solvers; and reach their goals. So why, when we're rolling out UDL as a school or district, do we serve up one-size-fits-all PD? When they provide no choices and do not attempt to build engagement, these PD sessions model the opposite of UDL. Isn't it ironic; don't you think?

UDL PD that channels the UDL principles celebrates and elevates teacher voices and empowers teachers to make choices about their professional learning. In this chapter, we discuss how to design professional development using the same principles that teachers use to design their lessons. This is critical, because if your goal is to move your school and district toward UDL, you will want to model it through your leadership practice. Often leaders will ask us, "What should I do as a first step in my UDL journey?" We advise: Model, model, model.

As you think about the power of professional learning to grow teachers' practice and create more equitable and inclusive systems, remember the motto "firm goals, flexible means." At the beginning of every meeting, you should be able to articulate what every staff member will know and be able to do as a result of the meeting. Too often, we have practices and procedures that are just part of "doing business" without really identifying specific goals and outcomes.

It is hard to forget a professional development session we once attended where a famous speaker and professor stood in front of us in the flesh . . . and played a video of herself speaking to us. There was nothing added to the video, such as graphics, to make it any more accessible or engaging. In fact, the distraction of watching the video while she stood there watching it with us made it much, much worse. Let's try to avoid a similar fate in our own leadership and learning.

Rome wasn't built in a day, and we certainly can't educate our kids in a day, nor our educators. All too often, our systems limit professional development for teachers to a single intensive day on a new program, initiative, or framework. An intensive PD day shouldn't be a single event, it should be part of a longer learning journey.

A single, intensive, professional development day can be a great way to get all staff members on the same page and build excitement and community around a new initiative. But we need to go further to help our teachers be successful. Just as we do for our students, we need to remove barriers for teachers, offer continuous support, and promote lifelong, expert learning that aligns with our core values.

Better UDL PD in Five Steps

So, how can you create better professional development for your educators? We've put together a list of five steps to help you with this process. Remember, you can't completely change your PD plan overnight, but when you try, try, and try again, you'll find that one day you'll look back and you won't recognize what's in your rearview mirror.

1. **Let Your Teachers Weigh In.** Your teachers need to have a voice in your education community. Every frustration, complaint, or issue is valid. Let your educators tell you what they need for professional development in order to reach the educator evaluation goals. Provide your teachers with a forum for sharing. In the spirit of UDL, allow them to choose the way they best communicate with you. For example, host a teachers' town hall, but also give teachers the option to complete an online form, send you an email, or have a conversation over the phone.

2. **Define Your Goals.** When we plan a PD session, we need to keep in mind what our goals are. Are you looking to build engagement, knowledge, or inspire your teachers into action? Are you launching a new initiative or building upon existing knowledge? Remember that UDL is always about "firm goals, flexible means." One great tip is to align these goals to your educator evaluation system rubric.

3. **Remove Barriers.** During step 1, you let your teachers define the barriers they face when teaching inclusive classrooms. Now it's your turn to think of other barriers that may interfere with your teachers' abilities to be successful. Come up with multiple pathways for addressing those barriers. Make sure to set aside the appropriate resources

(time/scheduling and funding) to alleviate some of the barriers. Let your educators know their concerns have been heard and what you plan to do. Even taking small steps can help show teachers that you value their opinions and are working in their best interest.

4. **Provide Choice.** Our teachers should have options, just as their students do, in how they learn. When delivering professional development, remember to provide multiple means of engagement, multiple means of representation, and multiple means of action and expression. By doing this, you will automatically eliminate many barriers (see step 3 above!). Maybe you start by hosting a school-wide or districtwide professional development day. But thereafter, what support will you provide to assist your teachers, particularly when you are introducing a new initiative or framework? Your district, school, and educator requirements will be unique, but we've compiled a list of some common additional supports:

   ● Instructional coaching and technical assistance

   ● Peer-to-peer groups

   ● Graduate-level courses (in person or online)

   ● Moderated book groups

   ● Faculty meetings

   ● At-home webinars

5. **Get Regular Feedback.** Listening isn't just a way to start a conversation about professional development. Listening should be a regular part of the learning process. When done frequently, you can learn what is working, what is not, and make course corrections. You can continue to remove barriers that you hadn't foreseen.

Create a community for your educators where feedback and open communication are welcomed and considered.

Given these steps, a model for the UDL transformation of the districtwide PD may look something like the process introduced in the book *Universally Designed Leadership* (Novak & Rodriguez, 2016), which is summarized here:

1. At the end of each school year, an electronic survey is distributed districtwide. Teachers are encouraged to request PD opportunities that would be most meaningful to them the following year based on the core values and a comprehensive data review.

2. Results of the annual survey are analyzed and a list of needed PD offerings is posted. Educators are encouraged to recommend professional development facilitators or apply to lead professional development in the identified areas. This allows exemplary educators to step into leadership roles and facilitate professional learning.

3. Teachers who are chosen to become leaders have the opportunity to showcase their skills to others. This also provides options for collaboration and community.

4. Presentation topics, session summaries, and agendas are announced early in the school year so that all educators can view their options and choices and register for the offerings that are meaningful, authentic, and relevant to them. This also supports educators in creating action plans for their professional practice goals.

5. After each session, the district sends out evaluation forms so participants can evaluate their experience to inform PD decisions for the next session. Also, presenters are given

valuable feedback on the effectiveness of the session to help them improve future offerings, which highlights the true meaning of voice and choice.

Exemplary teachers need leadership opportunities and a platform to help spread their awesomeness to others, and districts need more than one session to meet the needs of all educators. When we embrace UDL in our leadership practice, we embrace educators as leaders, which is also a great way to create an empowering school culture.

Professional Learning Communities

Following World War I, the United States sought to retreat into isolationism. Since the outside world was functioning so poorly, our government decided to focus on our own issues (of which there were plenty). A mere 20 years later, the problems of the world made their way to America anyway. The problems of the world were too big, and America was too influential to simply ignore them. Let this be a lesson for us as educators.

Even though it may be comfortable to be a great teacher in your own classroom, we are part of something larger. Being open to sharing with and learning from others is an integral part of a highly successful school and district. This also relates to the need for a strong culture in our schools. For many years teacher isolationism has been a barrier to growth in teaching. Many colleagues report that teachers are nervous or unwilling to share their thoughts, ideas, and materials with other teachers for a variety of reasons. Administrators cite this as a major obstacle for teacher growth.

Professional learning communities (PLCs) offer a collaborative approach to professional development in which small groups of educators meet regularly to reflect on instructional planning and practice, to share expertise and insights from their teaching experiences, and to engage in collective problem-solving (Ganias & Novak, 2020).

The UDL PLC structure promotes a continued professional learning opportunity for teachers to plan standards-based units of instruction, to incorporate student engagement and choice, to discuss applied practices, to review student work/data, and to offer each other feedback using a common framework. When participating in PLCs, educators generally examine four key questions (DuFour, DuFour, Eaker, & Many, 2010):

- What do we expect our students to learn?
- How will we know they are learning?
- How will we respond when they don't learn?
- How will we respond if they already know it?

These four questions provide a strong foundation for exploration and growth among educators but have the potential to lead to one-size-fits-all thinking. For example, when discussing "How will we know they are learning?" educators may create standardized assessments that prevent some students from sharing what they know. To rise above traditional pedagogical thinking, Ganias and Novak (2020) propose the following revisions to the questions to focus more on UDL:

- What do we expect our students to learn and why is it important?
- How can we design flexible assessments so students have multiple options to demonstrate their learning?
- If students do not learn, what potential barriers can we eliminate through thoughtful design?
- If students do learn, how will we provide options and choices to optimize challenge?

Another way to bring your professional learning communities to the next level includes focusing on co-planning and observation through lesson study. This requires openness and, at times, vulnerability, and it will definitely push staff to model giving and receiving mastery-oriented feedback. *Japanese lesson study* is one example of a practice that can broaden the scope of UDL in your school since learning from our peers is one of the most powerful tools in our PD toolbox. In Japanese lesson study, teachers with a common focus meet and plan lessons together (Doig & Groves, 2011). The lessons focus on building skills or understanding and are known as *research lessons*. They are taught by a single educator but observed by all of the teachers who participated in the planning, as well as additional educators. A debriefing session follows the lesson in which the lesson is discussed at some length and observers offer feedback and modifications.

The four phases of the lesson study include the following:

1. Goal-setting and planning, including developing the lesson plan;

2. Teaching the research lesson, enabling the lesson observation;

3. The post-lesson discussion; and

4. Resulting consolidation of learning, which has many far-reaching consequences.

Consider how professional learning communities could begin to incorporate co-planning and lesson study into meetings that drive the importance of universally designed instruction. For more information on facilitating a lesson study in your PLCs, we recommend the book *Stepping Up Lesson Study: An Educator's Guide to Deeper Learning* (Murata & Kim-Eng Lee, 2020).

Instructional Rounds

Not completely dissimilar from Japanese lesson study are *instructional rounds*. For this method to be successful, the same basic approach is needed; teachers must be willing to break free from an isolationist philosophy and be strong enough to be vulnerable. Whereas Japanese lesson study may focus more on the planning of lessons, instructional rounds focus on executing a planned lesson, and are more like a typical administrative observation, but without the pressure.

We have seen teachers begin to engage in peer observations on their own. If you have educators interested in instructional rounds, let them know that any time they wish to observe their peers (with permission from their peers, of course), you will do whatever you can to cover classes in order to make that a possibility. While observing peers is a wonderful and meaningful experience, formalizing the process with guidance takes it one step further.

With instructional rounds, teachers can visit classrooms in small groups. There is no set number of classes they must visit. A key item to highlight is that instructional rounds are not observations. Teachers will not be assessed and no teacher rubric or grading system is attached to the process. This simply provides teachers with opportunities to see other teachers in real classroom situations and then allows them to engage in the valuable opportunity to discuss what they saw with their peers.

If the teachers being observed are willing and comfortable, they may ask to hear feedback and ideas from the visiting teachers. Although there are plenty of formatted ways in which to engage in instructional rounds, it is important that the norms for this process are collectively determined and that all participants are comfortable with the process.

Here is an example of a protocol to inspire teachers to begin instructional rounds, although we always encourage them to personalize the process for their team.

——— Instructional Rounds Protocol ———

Before the day of the rounds, the lead teacher in each group will create a schedule that ensures that all teachers teach for 20 minutes and that there is adequate time for debrief.

1. The instructional rounds group will meet in the morning for 30 to 45 minutes to identify a problem of practice and corresponding focus questions to drive the day's observations. Here are some sample focus questions:

   ● How did the teacher provide multiple and varied options for student communication and expression?

   ● How did the teacher model and reinforce positive behavioral expectations?

   ● How did the teacher use data and student response to differentiate instruction and support?

2. The observation group makes the rounds into each group member's classroom to collect data related to the identified problem of practice (20 to 30 minutes per classroom) while observers make detailed, nonjudgmental notes regarding the focus question(s).

3. Debrief after each observation. The leader starts by reminding everyone that the purpose of the reflection/debrief is not to evaluate the observed teacher. Rules regarding how to share observations should be established prior to the debriefing. Useful rules include the following:

   ● Comments made during the debriefing should not be shared with anyone.

- ○ Do not offer suggestions to the observed teachers unless they explicitly ask for feedback.

- ○ Nothing observed within a lesson should be shared with anyone without permission.

4. Conduct a final debrief at the end of the day for 20 to 30 minutes to reflect on the process.

Share the instructional rounds process at a staff meeting. The team decides what they are comfortable sharing. Focus on the value of the process as job-embedded professional development and how it would improve all teachers' practice.

Rejuvenating the Faculty Meeting

Another opportunity you have to design and deliver professional learning is in your faculty meetings. Yep, that's right. Universally designed meetings. Many schools focus on inclusive practice and equity through the lens of UDL in classrooms. In these schools, evaluators are looking in classrooms for students to have voice and choice so they can personalize their learning. The irony is that sometimes when you walk into a faculty meeting in these schools you will see a traditional passive "sit and get" approach.

Possibly, a principal has prepared a slideshow and asked the entire staff to read a hard copy of an article or look at data while following the same protocol. If we are going to move away from one-size-fits-all teaching and learning, we have to acknowledge that our teachers will be more empowered and engaged if we provide them with autonomy and self-advocacy as they participate in meaningful learning experiences.

Transitioning from the traditional to the more effective is as difficult for administrators as it is for classroom teachers. To be honest, faculty meetings may be easier to plan when you simply put an agenda out and share information with your staff. They are also less effective. Staff meetings created with UDL in mind involve much more. Sometimes they may look like collaborative efforts, sometimes they involve choice activities with sharing afterward, and yes, sometimes, in the interest of time management, they are just venues for administrators simply to share some pertinent information.

Faculty meetings are essential in our school culture. Depending on the district and structures set forth through teacher contracts, you probably only get the entire faculty together once or twice a month. Begin to be a more effective leader by making adjustments in how you approach routine events like staff meetings. As an example, we encourage administrators to specifically set aside time in faculty meetings for faculty educators to present new and interesting practices that they are using in their classrooms. Consider using groups to work through mandatory training information. When possible, provide multiple ways in which the staff can access necessary information as well. For example, instead of reading the same article about UDL, offer options to read an article, listen to a podcast, or watch a short video.

High-quality professional development is critical to shift teacher practices and increase student learning. When you, as a leader, examine your PD for potential barriers and design offerings using UDL as a lens and a framework, you can increase choice and voice among staff members and ensure that you embody the importance of "firm goals, flexible means" in your leadership practice. Consider the following actions as you begin to transition your own professional development models to a model that increases engagement and results in expert learning.

- Consider how professional learning communities could begin to incorporate co-planning and lesson study into meetings that drive the importance of universally designed instruction.

◗ At your next faculty meeting, whether in person or remote (or if you give teachers a choice!), ask teachers what kind of professional development would be most meaningful for their own practice. Allow them to share their thoughts with each other and ask interested parties if they would like to join a professional development committee to create an action plan to provide more options and choices. Don't forget to provide multiple means of action and expression!

◗ Give your teachers a feedback survey after the next professional development session. Consider providing them with an open-ended sentence starter that will bring your practice to the next level. "The next time, it would be cool if . . ." is a great one. If you collect the feedback, be sure to share it with them at the next meeting!

Self-Reflection Questions for Leaders

1. How skilled are you at universally designing professional development for your colleagues? If you tend to provide one-size-fits-all professional development, how can you begin to transition to UDL?

2. How can you leverage effective teaching and teachers as a form of professional development through PLCs, lesson study, instructional rounds, and so on?

3. What is your current model of professional development and how does it align to what you have learned in this chapter about how to universally design ongoing professional development?

5

Educator Evaluation to Improve Teacher Efficacy

Universally designed leadership requires us to model expert learning and support all stakeholders in their own professional growth. While providing professional learning in UDL practices can help us create more inclusive and equitable systems, we need to do more. We must support and elevate teacher practice through a system of educator evaluation. If we believe in equity and inclusion, we need to ensure that all learners have equal access to high-quality curriculum and teaching that meets their needs and helps them to achieve at high levels. To do this, we need to provide feedback to teachers so we can optimize UDL in their practice.

As instructional leaders, we must make it a priority to give educators mastery-oriented feedback about their teaching. To do this, we need to create valuable feedback loops through the educator evaluation cycle. In each cycle, this feedback loop can be compared to the research process, commencing with the question "Is my support effective in increasing the outcomes of all staff members and students?" and moving through the phases of measurement, analysis, and reflection. This process is ongoing and is reiterated many times (Venning & Buisman-Pijlman, 2013). To simplify, feedback loops consistently answer the following questions:

1. What are our goals?
2. Where are we now? (How will we measure that?)
3. How will we get everyone to where we want to go? (How will we measure that?)

We need to analyze how our goals for teachers align with UDL and our core values. We also need to answer one of the biggest, most pressing questions facing us every Monday morning: "How will we get everyone to where we want to go?" Let's further examine the three questions as we think about creating inclusive, equitable classrooms through the process of educator evaluation.

What Are Our Goals?

Before instruction begins, educators need to determine the end goal. Teachers use state standards to design instruction. As administrators, we use teacher educator evaluation rubrics to determine the goals we have for teacher performance. Since teachers are evaluated using a rubric adopted by the district or state, that rubric should be aligned to the expectations and values of UDL. In some schools, it may be a valuable exercise to create a crosswalk between the UDL Guidelines (udlguidelines.cast.org) and educator evaluation rubrics to find the overlap between the two, to deepen teachers' understanding of UDL principles, and to heighten teachers' own awareness of the standards by which they will be evaluated.

Teachers today are required to implement inclusive practices. Yet, many of our educator evaluation systems continue to emphasize one-size-fits-all teaching practices that do not match up with our expectations of teachers. If personalization is so important, why aren't our educator evaluation systems measuring that? In a study published by the Center on Teacher Quality, a list of recommendations for overhauling educator evaluation included the following (Center for Teaching Quality, 2013):

> We all agree that evaluation systems have an important role to play in making every teacher more effective. "Drive-by" evaluations are all too common in many schools, and even those are too infrequent to offer the kind of feedback teachers need to grow as professionals.

As school and district leaders, it is our responsibility to provide mastery-oriented feedback to teachers through a robust educator evaluation system. As with UDL curriculum planning, we need to begin with our goals for teachers and where we want them to be. Although we don't have state standards for effective teaching, we do have frameworks that provide clear evidence of what we should be seeing in classrooms.

Many districts and states align their systems of evaluation to research completed by Charlotte Danielson. Her *Framework for Teaching* has become the most widely used definition of teaching in the United States and has been adopted as the single model, or one of several approved models, in over 30 states (The Danielson Group, 2020). The four domains of professional practice include these:

- ➔ Planning and Preparation
- ➔ Classroom Environment
- ➔ Instruction
- ➔ Professional Responsibilities

Under each of these domains, there are specific outcomes, or standards, for teacher practice. For example, when designing instruction, the Danielson Framework offers the following description of practice that is "highly effective":

> The sequence of learning activities follows a coherent sequence, is aligned to instructional goals, and is designed to engage students in high-level cognitive activity. These are appropriately

differentiated for individual learners. Instructional groups are varied appropriately, with some opportunity for student choice.

Now, tell us: How is it possible for a teacher to exemplify highly effective practice without the UDL framework? Through UDL, teachers are urged to design instruction that "heightens the salience of goals and objectives" (CAST, 2018). They are called to design with student engagement in mind. Collaboration and community need to be a part of classroom culture, and most importantly, students are empowered to make choices about their learning. Be honest, how many educators do you think are marked as being "highly effective" who don't actually exemplify that practice? We don't know the answer, but we know it's not zero.

In your school or district, you have an amazing opportunity as a leader to highlight the importance of using the principles of UDL for planning and preparing learning experiences that allow all educators to create a classroom environment that is engaging, authentic, challenging, and supportive for all students. We have to hold our teachers to the highest of expectations, as it's our job to ensure they meet the goals outlined in the educator evaluation system.

If your rubric is not explicitly aligned to UDL, we assure you that the alignment is there implicitly. We have yet to see an educator evaluation rubric that did not require the UDL framework to achieve its goal. So, how do you know?

Look for some keywords that will help you to see the connection. If your educator evaluation uses any of the following words, and all students don't have equal opportunities to succeed, then get your UDL design hat on and get ready to roll:

- Autonomy
- Collaboration
- Differentiation
- Engagement
- Reflection
- Self-Advocacy
- Variety

Where Are We Now?

In order to design your support for educators and increase the level of UDL mastery-oriented feedback, you have to have a clear starting point. You can use a number of tools to measure the level of UDL implementation in your classrooms. The most critical step is ensuring that all teachers have a voice in selecting the tool and measurement and how it will be used to determine growth, differentiate support, and increase the outcomes of students.

Let's discuss three tools: the UDL Progression Rubric, the UDL Implementation Rubric, and the tool adapted from Olofson et al. (2018) used to measure the level of implementation for personalized learning.

UDL Progression Rubric

The UDL Progression Rubric (Novak & Rodriguez, 2018), shared in the appendix, can be an important link to continuing the progress of UDL implementation in your school or district. Keep in mind that, like our students, all of our teachers learn differently. Simply explaining what UDL is and providing some teachers with a link to the Guidelines may be enough to get them moving in the right direction. Some teachers may need some scaffolding to clarify for them what UDL in practice really looks like. The UDL Progression Rubric provides examples of what UDL looks like in each of the UDL Guidelines. Does it cover everything that could be utilized? No, that would be impossible, but it does provide what teachers are often looking for, which is some sort of real, tangible example of how to get started, how to progress, and, finally, how to become an expert, UDL-based educator.

UDL Implementation Rubric

After reviewing the UDL Progression Rubric (Figure 5.1), you probably recognize that UDL isn't a framework that you can implement overnight. It takes years—not weeks or months—to reach expert level, and it's easy to see how anyone, even the most experienced teachers, could get overwhelmed. For those just getting started, evaluating where you are in the UDL implementation process on a checkpoint-by-checkpoint basis might simply be too much.

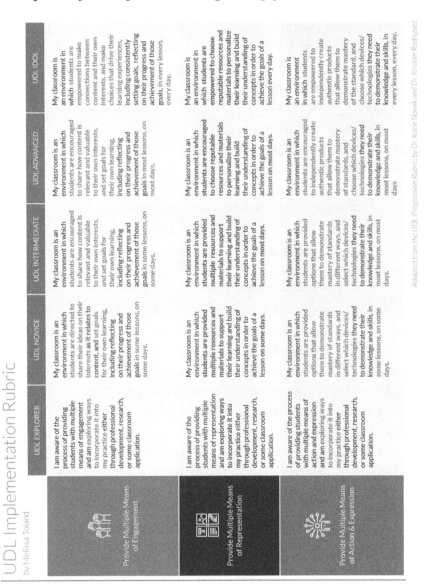

Figure 5.1: The UDL Implementation Rubric

When Melissa Toland of Ocean View School District in Oxnard, CA, reached out suggesting a simplified version for the time-strapped or overwhelmed teacher, we were totally sold. This rubric is a great tool for self-evaluation and self-reflection in regard to big picture UDL implementation, and it also serves as a fantastic reference tool for remembering overall themes of UDL. When you are ready to get a little more granular, the UDL Progression Rubric builds upon this one.

Measure Teacher Practices to Support Personalized Learning

To measure the school's implementation of UDL, you may want to use a measurement tool to determine whether students have opportunities to personalize their learning to meet rigorous standards by choosing methods, materials, and assessment options that both challenge and support them.

Building on Olofson et al. (2018), we offer the following baseline of observation prompts to help you provide feedback, design professional learning, and set lead measures for improvement:

- Teacher provides numerous opportunities for students to identify their own strengths and needs and to self-assess (e.g., reflect, analyze) to personalize their own learning.

- Teacher appreciates and uses learners' personal, family, and community experiences when providing students with options and choices.

- Teacher creates opportunities to ensure that students develop the skills needed for successful collaborative group work.

- Teacher creates opportunities for students to use technology to pursue learning goals and standards and to generate evidence of proficiency in multiple ways (e.g., videos, podcasts, dynamic presentations).

How Will We Get Everyone to Where We Want to Go?

The crux of improvement is the quality of the feedback and guidance we provide so that teachers can improve their practice. We imagine all teachers are receiving feedback, but are they receiving the right kind? In the book *Thanks for the Feedback*, Stone and Heen (2015) name three types of feedback: appreciation, evaluation, and coaching.

All three types of feedback have their place as we prepare for UDL implementation, but each type of feedback has very different purposes. The purpose of *appreciation* is to increase motivation, improve culture, and make people feel good. This is absolutely necessary, but it is not adequate to increase or improve performance. If someone says to you, "Your apple pie is absolutely amazing. Seriously, I've never eaten anything so delicious," you are going to be super motivated to bake another pie for that person, but you won't change the recipe *at all*. In short, appreciation gives you more of the same, which is why it is so critical to praise performance that is truly worthy of praise or the effort that you see.

Carol Dweck (2006), a psychology researcher at Stanford University, coined the term *growth mindset*. She writes: "In a growth mindset, people believe that their most basic abilities can be developed through dedication and hard work—brains and talent are just the starting point. This view creates a love of learning and a resilience that is essential for great accomplishments" (p. iii).

Evaluation such as ratings, grades, and judgments on rubrics can help people understand where they are. Such evaluations can aid in self-reflection and provide an objective view of where we stand. However, if the one receiving the feedback thinks it is off-base, unfair, or poorly delivered (even if it isn't any of those things), they will ignore it and not use it to grow or improve (Stone & Heen, 2015).

When teachers are not meeting the needs of all students, you need to provide clear, actionable feedback to this point, even when it's hard to give and harder for teachers to hear. The UDL literature refers to this *coaching* type of feedback as *mastery-oriented feedback*. Even the thickest skinned of us can feel like crawling into a cave when we hear a piece of negative feedback. But mastery-oriented feedback is necessary for growth and improvement, and we have to provide it.

Think back to the apple pie. Let's say that pie was good, but not great. Start your feedback with a touch of appreciation, add in an evaluation, and move on to coaching: "This apple pie is yummy—I'd say an eight out of ten—but the apples are a little crunchy. Next time, maybe you could try using a different type of apple or cook it for 5 to 10 minutes longer, and it will be the perfect texture." Using the three types of feedback together allow us to praise effort, provide an objective view of where teachers are in relationship to the goals based on observations of practice, and supply high-quality feedback about possible next steps. So, what does this look like?

Creating Teacher Feedback That Targets UDL

Although different requirements may be present in different districts, it is sometimes helpful to see how others may provide feedback from a typical teacher observation using the UDL framework and the three types of feedback. Remember that teacher feedback through evaluation often carries a negative connotation for obvious reasons. Evaluation may, of course, be used to identify weaknesses in teachers, but our job as administrators is to provide feedback, coaching, and ongoing support so that teachers can work toward rigorous goals set in the teacher rubric. You can minimize the threat and distraction of providing targeted feedback in numerous ways including by building meaningful relationships, by providing the option to meet face to face to discuss, and by encouraging teachers to provide you with feedback about your leadership practices.

In this scenario, imagine that a principal observes a social studies teacher who is asking students to respond to a document-based question. The district has just introduced UDL, and the principal wants to encourage teachers while also helping them to see areas where they could continue to eliminate barriers to learning. Students are working in small groups when the principal comes in.

There is a standard written on the board: "Cite specific textual evidence to support analysis of primary and secondary sources, attending to such features as the date and origin of the information."

In the lesson, students are given access to three primary source documents and then they must answer the question "Which account do you find most believable? Why?" The principal observes the lesson for 10 minutes and writes the following:

Ms. Smith utilized a teaching strategy that is meant to better motivate and engage her students. Students were given instructions to work in groups to complete their document comparison work. Before students formed groups, Ms. Smith helped to minimize threats and distractions by reminding students to make sure they don't leave anyone out and asked students to share strategies for creating inclusive groups where everyone is a part of the classroom community. Taking the time to address potential barriers was an effective choice to engage students. As students were working, she reminded them to self-assess a thesis. Ms. Smith explained that many students probably are not familiar with doing this yet and she had organized some resources for students to reference to acquaint themselves with how to write a thesis, including effective examples. She offered them the choice of logging in to Google Classroom, where she had posted a number of resources on thesis writing, or accessing paper copies of similar documents that she had in the classroom. Providing students with choices in their acquisition of content/skills and in assessments is key to allowing students the optimal manner in which to get the information and show their ability to meet a given standard. This demonstrates an "emerging" engagement strategy in the UDL Progression Rubric.

Moving forward, it would be great if Ms. Smith's students could have multiple means to access the primary source documents. For example, some students may have difficulty decoding, so providing the documents online would allow students to use Google to translate documents into their first language or have the documents read to them. Ms. Smith will want to keep that in mind the next time she provides reading materials. Since she already uses Google Classroom, she could post links there.

Providing the mastery-oriented feedback at the end allows for a great discussion point at a follow-up conference. Have a copy of the UDL Progression Rubric handy at your meeting and discuss what it would take to move from "emerging" to "proficient" in the UDL checkpoint "Optimizing choice and autonomy." Brainstorming together on this can take away the perceived punitive nature of evaluation for many teachers. It also helps to set the stage to avoid defensiveness, especially when you add, "How can I support you so you can try this? If you'd like, I could model a lesson for you."

If you observe practices that are truly exemplary, you want to make sure that you still provide mastery-oriented feedback. As an example, as UDL in the classroom grows in scope and quality in your school or district, you can utilize the evaluation tool to find educators modeling UDL practices, praise them, and ask them to share their experiences with colleagues.

The following sample observation write-up shows how to help support collaboration and community in the teaching staff. In this fictional class, the teacher asked students to describe how the characters respond or change as the plot moves toward a resolution.

Ms. Smith demonstrates expert knowledge of the developmental levels of fourth graders and uses the knowledge to differentiate learning experiences that allow the students to exercise self-management, make decisions, and make significant progress toward meeting intended outcomes. During this observation, Ms. Smith introduced the unit on characterization and outlined the upcoming assessment. Ms. Smith provided students with choices to allow them to make decisions regarding their own learning. Students were told they would have the autonomy to choose whom to work with, which book they would use, what type of presentation they would make, what type of visual they would use, as well as a type of soundtrack for their presentation. When helping students to select books, Ms. Smith encouraged visits to the library, graphic novels, audio books, short stories, and screenplays. One student asked, "Can I bring in a book from home that I am reading?" and she responded with, "Of course you can. What are you reading? I need a good book!" Students who learn in different ways or have varied interests would have a greater likelihood of making connections to the content of this lesson than in a typical/traditional lesson. Students were also provided with self-assessment checklists and rubrics so that they could assess their own performance and effort as they work through the project as well as with Peer Assessment Rubrics to help them determine the effectiveness of the collaborations they choose.

As a result, the students in this class appeared to genuinely be excited about the unit and tasks for this lesson, could identify the main purpose of the assignment, and could meet the expectations of the standard. Ms. Smith is demonstrating proficiency in "Optimize individual choice and autonomy." Overall, this lesson met many of the expectations for proficient practice. It would be amazing for all staff members to see how Ms. Smith designed the unit. It would be great if she would be willing to demonstrate and share the lesson at the beginning of the next faculty meeting as a model of effective practice.

When we follow up with this teacher, we would be looking to gain insight into the preparation process that got her to this point.

Here is another great opportunity to brainstorm and look for ways to push this even further. The best teachers are always looking for ways to improve their practice. It is just as important to assist this teacher in pushing forward as it is a struggling teacher or the teacher in the first example who is emerging as a promising educator. Further, when we identify teachers who demonstrate proficient or expert UDL practice through observations and evaluations, we need to provide them with opportunities to become teacher leaders and model their practice for their colleagues. Some may be reluctant to do so at first but having in-house UDL adopters available is an essential strategy in creating ongoing professional learning.

If exemplary educators are reluctant or uncomfortable in presenting to an entire faculty, find some way to share the expertise that you have witnessed. Here are some ideas to support and grow your most proficient teachers:

- ➲ Ask them if they would be willing to meet with new teachers in a small group setting to share some of their ideas and experience.
- ➲ Ask them to present at a department meeting where they may be more comfortable.
- ➲ Ask them if they would be comfortable having part of their class filmed to share with others.
- ➲ Ask them if they would be comfortable having their ideas and success shared by an administrator at a faculty meeting.

Think UDL. Provide them with as many choices as you need to reach your goals of establishing teachers in your building as UDL leaders. You need them to make this work!

If you have an opportunity to review teacher lesson plans as a component of educator evaluation, you can also use your UDL lens. Boxing legend Mike Tyson once said, "Everyone has a plan until they get punched in the mouth." Sometimes a boxing ring and a classroom can be very similar. We know we will all agree that at the end of some days it feels like we have gone 10 rounds with a professional fighter. We need a plan, but we also need a plan on how to handle those things we haven't planned for.

When we are examining a lesson plan or talking with teachers in preconferences leading up to an observation, we want to see a strong plan but also want to see a level of self-awareness in the planning, showing that the teacher knows they are not going to reach everyone with one strategy. We like to see some "What if?" thinking. Teachers in California see these self-reflective questions at the top of each element of the California Standards for the Teaching Profession (CSTP) (Commission on Teacher Credentialing, 2009).

——— "How Do I . . ." or "Why Do I . . ." ———

- ⊃ Systematically check for student understanding and revise plans accordingly?

- ⊃ Incorporate a variety of strategies in a lesson to check for student understanding?

- ⊃ Monitor the learning of students with limited English proficiency or of students with special needs?

- ⊃ Adjust the lesson plan to accelerate instruction when I determine that the pace of the lesson is too slow?

- ⊃ Make "on the spot" changes in my lesson based on students' interests and questions?

- ⊃ Provide additional support and opportunities for students to learn when some students have mastered the lesson objective(s) and others have not?

- ⊃ Adjust my lesson when I don't have enough time to complete everything I planned to do?

Urge teachers to keep these types of questions in mind when they are planning. Once we begin with "What if?" thinking, we are more prepared to meet our students at a place where they can access the curriculum more effectively.

In this chapter, you have learned why educator evaluation is so critical for implementing UDL. You have an amazing opportunity to help heighten the importance of educator evaluation as you provide ongoing feedback to all staff members. The following next steps may help to support your teachers in their implementation of UDL:

- ➲ Begin to unpack your educator evaluation rubric with your leadership team. Create a UDL crosswalk.

- ➲ Reflect on the observations you write for your educators. Take one out and compare/contrast to the sample observations in this chapter. Are you explicit about your expectations for the implementation of UDL? If not, where in the observation write-up could you have made that clearer?

- ➲ Review a teacher lesson plan. Are there options and choices in the methods, materials, and assessments? If so, how can you encourage the teacher to become a teacher leader to help colleagues? If not, how can you provide feedback, professional development, and/or support to improve the design of the lessons?

- ➲ Encourage a culture of mutual feedback with your teachers. Ask how you can provide them with more helpful feedback and support.

Self-Reflection Questions for Leaders

1. What are the biggest barriers for you as an administrator when providing educator evaluation to your teachers? How can you set different expectations or develop a culture to help overcome those barriers?

2. How does your existing educator evaluation system align to the UDL Guidelines? Do you think providing a cross-walk between the Guidelines and your educator evaluation rubric would be helpful?

3. Think of a time when you provided unhelpful feedback at work or in your personal life—for example, praise for something you didn't like. After reading this chapter, how could you provide mastery-oriented feedback in that situation? How do you think your feedback would have been met?

6

All Things Curriculum

As educational leaders, we have to ensure that all learners access curriculum and teaching that is relevant, authentic, and meaningful. To do this, we need a firm understanding of what curriculum entails and how we can design, adopt, and revise curriculum through the lens of UDL.

UDL is focused on four core components of curriculum: goals, methods, materials, and assessments. In *Universal Design for Learning: Theory and Practice*, Meyer, Rose, and Gordon (2014) note, "This definition of curriculum is broader than a traditional one which treats curriculum as a sequence of content elements conveyed by a particular set of instructional materials. We emphasize the interconnectedness of these four components and emphasize the importance of goals and assessment in designing effective curriculum" (p. 68).

Grace Meo (2008), one of the cofounders of CAST, where the UDL framework was developed, further discusses the importance of ensuring that all four components of the curriculum are designed with the lens of UDL: "Bringing UDL into classrooms and educational practice may sound like a difficult task, and it is, if a classroom is guided by vaguely defined goals and equipped with only conventional instructional methods, traditional materials (e.g., textbooks and pencils), and inflexible options for demonstrating knowledge and understanding (e.g., written responses, either essay or multiple choice)" (p. 22).

In Chapter 3, we showed that the UDL principles drive design by rooting the design of teaching and learning with three core questions:

- ◑ What is it that all learners need to know or be able to do?

- ◑ Based on variability, what barriers may prevent students from learning?

- ◑ How do I design flexible pathways for all learners to learn and share what they know?

These pathways should include flexibility in the design of the goals, methods, materials, and assessments. Without asking these questions throughout the design process, we are apt to slip into tried-and-true practices that are one-size-fits-all, which will make the implementation of UDL difficult, as Meo noted.

Take this unfortunate but memorable lesson from Mike's college days on the importance of clear, firm goals that can be achieved by flexible means. As he was looking to finish up his college degree in economics, Mike enrolled in a senior seminar class that culminated in the writing of an essay. The essay had to be at least 30 pages on the economic system of any country in the world. There was very little else given in the way of particulars for this assignment: no rubric, no exemplar, no opportunities for collaboration or feedback, no guiding questions. The only clear expectation: 30 pages.

Mike was determined to meet that goal. Given the opportunity to choose a country, he picked the one with the longest name because writing it over and over would take up a lot of precious white space. Let the other students have France and Spain, Mike chose Czechoslovakia.

Keep in mind that by this time, in the mid-1990s, Czechoslovakia was splitting into two countries: the Czech Republic and

Slovakia. The only familiar fact about this country's economy that Mike was aware of was that most of the hockey pucks he had seen were manufactured there. You would not believe how many sentences could start with Czechoslovakia or the former Czechoslovakia or the countries of Slovakia and the Czech Republic! In the end, 30 pages were filled, and graduation did in fact occur about a month later. But the vague and underwhelming goal for that assignment left a lasting impression—and not a good one—on this future educator.

How can we support our teaching staff to design curriculum that is relevant, authentic, and meaningful? We discussed professional learning and educator evaluation in previous chapters, but within each of those pathways, we need to provide support for curriculum design. We can do this by focusing on the core questions of the UDL design process.

Core Question 1. What do all learners need to know or be able to do? When infusing UDL into systems, educators must be clear about what learners should know or be able to do in Tier 1 classrooms. Is there a clear scope and sequence? What are the essential or power standards?

Once standards are identified, they should be consistently shared with learners to support expert learning, self-regulation, and self-reflection. For example, when you are observing classrooms and evaluating teachers, encourage teachers to heighten the salience of goals and objectives by sharing the goal or standard with the students. It should be crystal clear to all learners, "When this lesson or unit is over, you will all know, or be able to do [insert goal]."

Core Question 2. Based on variability, what barriers may prevent students from learning? Identifying barriers is an ongoing process that requires us to ask for feedback, collaborate with learners, and practice reflection. In inclusive classrooms, all students have access to grade-level learning experiences that are both challenging and supportive. Sometimes, there are barriers that prevent all students from being educated together. If that is the case, administrators have to support teachers to eliminate them. Recent research argues:

> The barriers to learning and participation have different natures and can occur at different levels such as the attitudinal, the organizational and the contextual. For this reason, it is essential that professionals in the field of education are aware of their existence, know how to identify them and are capable of proposing changes and improvements that eliminate them in order to offer inclusive responses to students (Arnaiz Sánchez, de Haro Rodríguez, & Maldonado Martínez, 2019, p. 18).

When thinking about predictable barriers, the following considerations adapted from the UDL Guidelines may help educators to understand the variability of learners and anticipate the barriers present in inclusive learning environments. These suggested considerations are just a beginning, not a comprehensive list. Feel free to add your own.

When considering engagement:

- Students may not be interested by content.
- Students may lack prerequisite knowledge, skills, or motivation to continue to persist when there is significant challenge.
- Students may struggle with self-regulation and expected behaviors.
- Curriculum may not be culturally sustaining.

When considering comprehension/learning:

- Students may not be able to perceive instruction if only a single modality is used (overreliance on lecture, or text, for example).

○ Students may struggle to comprehend the language or symbols used in the learning environment.

○ Students may lack critical background knowledge that allows them to build comprehension.

When considering how students will express what they know/complete assessments:

○ Students may struggle to complete tasks without assistive technology or access to manipulatives, opportunities to move, etc.

○ Students may struggle to express what they know if given a single modality without adequate scaffolding.

○ Some students may struggle with executive functioning.

Core Question 3. How do I design flexible pathways for all learners to learn and share what they know? Once teachers can identify firm goals and potential barriers to reaching them, they can begin to think of flexible pathways to eliminate those barriers through design. Having flexible pathways doesn't mean that educators should do away with direct, explicit instruction. As you support educators in your practice, remember that explicit instruction, when brief and universally designed, can provide a solid foundation for self-differentiated learning.

Explicit instruction often includes clear and direct explanations, teacher modeling, and scaffolded prompts and questioning designed to gradually release responsibility for independent strategy selection (Morano et al., 2020). Given that we want all students to become expert learners who take ownership of their learning, providing explicit instruction can be a valuable instructional strategy, as long as barriers to this instruction are eliminated.

Although the specifics of direct, explicit, and whole-class instruction may vary, many practitioners agree that a mini-lesson should last no more than 10 to 15 minutes, and should contain four basic components: connection, teaching, active engagement, and link.

- **Connection:** Teachers share from the beginning how the goal is relevant, authentic, and meaningful to students.

- **Teaching:** Although UDL is a learner-centered approach, teacher-directed instruction can provide important scaffolding before students are ready to become more independent and to personalize their learning. Teachers should not, however, rely on a single representation. For example, if the teacher prepares a lecture, they would also offer visual or multimedia alternatives to support understanding as well as provide access to translation tools, assistive technology, and opportunities for students to ask questions.

- **Active Engagement:** Teachers provide students with an opportunity to *do* something, such as an informal, formative assessment. For example, if the teacher modeled two math problems, the students are asked to complete their own—with options, of course, to work with a partner, use a model, and/or use manipulatives.

- **Link:** Teachers are crystal clear about linking back to the goal and then directing students to applied practice or more independent work. For example, you may hear, "Now that you understand the goal of the lesson today, you will have an opportunity to make a choice about how to better understand the topic . . ."

After the mini-lesson, students are engaged in self-differentiated learning that optimizes engagement with methods, materials, and assessments. Teachers may set this up as stations, in a hyperlink document, or by simply sharing with the students what options they have. Remember that there are numerous flexible pathways for students to build knowledge. For example, a teacher may provide the following options for students to self-differentiate their learning.

- Read or listen to a text (textbook, primary source document, article, etc.).
- Watch a video or listen to a podcast.
- Access additional teacher direct instruction.

Once students participate in self-differentiated learning, teachers can provide a formative assessment so students can share what they have learned. When designing assessments, teachers must consider exactly what students need to know and do—but not limit the specific methods or means they use to demonstrate that knowledge or skill. Here are some assessment tips that may be valuable as you provide professional learning and feedback to educators.

- Teachers may start with a traditional assessment and ask students to propose other ways of showing that they met the standard or additional resources they need to complete it. An assignment choice slip may be approved before beginning assessment.
- The teacher may brainstorm numerous options for students to consider when sharing what they have learned (sonnet, screenplay, blog, vlog, essay, multimedia presentation, etc.). Teachers can provide the list and ask students to reflect and determine if any are appropriate options to share that they met the standard.
- Even if every student receives the same assessment, a teacher can provide options and choices for using scaffolds and supports. Encourage teachers to provide access to graphic organizers, exemplars, accessibility devices

(Read&Write for Google Chrome), math reference sheets, their notes, and so forth.

◑ Teachers encourage revisions and retakes after students reflect and explore additional resources to encourage perseverance.

In universally designed classrooms, more focus should be placed on diagnostic and formative assessments than on summative assessments. One aspect of being an expert learner is self-reflection. In order for educators to determine the effectiveness of their instruction, they need frequent formative assessments, which are "assessments for learning: tools that provide teachers with actionable information about their students and the practice in real time" (Rothman & Jobs for the Future, 2018, p. 4).

Once students have learned material through access to a universally designed curriculum, teachers can give summative assessments, which measure a student's growth since the beginning of the unit. For those who do not show adequate growth, Tier 2 intervention may be necessary to catch them up before moving on to more complex topics.

Curriculum Adoption

In the previous section, we discussed how teachers can improve a curriculum with UDL approaches. That said, we recognize that many educators may have a curriculum, or may be looking to adopt a curriculum that already provides goals, methods, materials, and assessments.

Adopted curriculum can be a helpful resource for teachers. We like to think about teaching and learning a little like construction. To build a house, you need both a skilled contractor and high-quality tools. Without tools, a truly skilled builder would likely be resourceful and find a way to build a house. But without a builder, a house simply won't be built, despite how many tools are available at the job site. High-quality curriculum resources are those tools, and educators are the builders of lessons that need to meet the needs of all students.

We love the guidance from Council of the Great City Schools (2017) in its report *Supporting Excellence: A Framework for Developing, Implementing, and Sustaining a High-Quality District Curriculum*:

> The district curriculum is not a textbook or a set of materials. An effective curriculum does, however, identify and connect educators to resources that the district requires, and provides guidance in the selection and use of classroom resources. The curriculum considers the time required to teach the essential content to all students. Feedback from users is incorporated in the development, revision, and implementation of the district curriculum to leverage teacher expertise and to ensure continuous reflection and refinement of the district's instructional principles and expectations (p. 2).

We have also found that successful UDL implementation depends on critical feedback from users to guide the revision of curriculum in ways that will meet the needs of all learners. So, although a high-quality curriculum is an incredible resource, its adoption must be understood as a tool for teachers—but not as a mere script that is expected to work for all learners. We have to empower teachers to, in turn, inspire, empower, and engage the students in their classrooms.

Steps for Review and/or Adoption

Here is the protocol we designed for curriculum design and review in our district. Consider how you could use or revise it in your own setting as you provide educators with the tools they need to universally design instruction for all learners.

1. Establish a review committee that will oversee the review or adoption process, including teachers who will be using

the curriculum and/or textbooks. Encourage students and parents to serve on the review committee.

2. Have the review committee meet to identify values and critical considerations to guide the review and/or adoption process. If you have core values, it is critical to align to these. The committee will create a timeline for review and/or adoption and share it with administrators. If there is an adoption, the timeline includes a pilot, and the duration of the pilot must be clear.

3. Next, the committee develops a rubric to review programs based on the critical considerations they selected (see the sample rubric that follows). The committee can revise as necessary. Please note that during the procedure, teachers must review all educational materials for simplistic and demeaning generalizations on the basis of race, color, sex, gender identity, religion, national origin, and sexual orientation. *Note: If any generalizations are present and the curriculum is selected for adoption, appropriate activities, discussions, and/or supplementary materials must be used to provide balance and context for any such stereotypes depicted in such materials. This is required by Civil Rights law.*

4. The committee selects at least two programs to review and contacts vendors to request sample materials.

5. Once materials arrive, the committee reviews and scores selected program texts using their rubric.

6. If they are not already represented on the committee, teachers who are expected to teach the curriculum will meet and discuss the merits of each of the sample programs and/or supplemental materials through the lens of UDL.

7. After review, the committee selects programs that will be piloted. The committee will also define the length and

expectations of the pilot. *Note: During a pilot, all materials should be implemented with fidelity to determine if any changes will need to be made when adopted. Once barriers are identified, the adoption team can consider how UDL will provide more access and engagement for all students when the program is adopted.*

8. Assessment data and feedback from teachers and students will be gathered throughout the pilot stage. *Note: It's valuable at this stage to allow multiple stakeholders to review materials and give feedback. You may consider an open forum for parents and community members to review materials and provide feedback.*

9. After the pilot stage, the committee makes a recommendation to the administrative team to adopt a program based on staff, student, and community feedback.

10. Together with the administrative team, the committee develops a sustained plan for professional development for teachers who will use the program so the program aligns to the district vision for eliminating inequities and ensuring that all students have opportunities to become expert learners in inclusive classrooms.

11. The administrative team confirms pricing, including shipping and all supplemental materials, for the selected program.

12. The selected program, the adoption process and timeline, the plan for professional development, and all associated costs are presented to the school committee.

13. The process of purchasing the adopted program and supplemental materials will be completed. Teachers will be offered professional development to work with the new program.

——Curriculum Adoption Sample Rubric——

Rate each textbook series being evaluated on a scale of 0 to 3:

   3 = Superior

   2 = Good

   1 = Fair

   0 = Poor, or feature not present

	Program 1	Program 2	Program 3
Suitability			
Reading level is appropriate for students and/or scaffolded with rich visuals and explicit vocabulary instruction.			
There are no generalizations in the text on the basis of race, color, sex, gender identity, religion, national origin, and sexual orientation.			
Content matches grade-level state standards.			
Strategies			
Emphasis on critical thinking/problem solving and expert learning			
Multiple/varied instructional activities focused on student self-differentiation			
Provision for small group study and collaboration			
Characteristics			
Number/clarity of visuals including charts, diagrams, illustrations, graphic organizers, etc. that provide multiple means of representation to learners			

	Program 1	Program 2	Program 3
Support materials			
Teacher's guide that provides support for providing options and choices for scaffolding and additional challenge			
Assessment package that provides multiple means of expression			
Online resources that students can access to customize the display of information			
Total points			

UDL Curriculum Makeover

Now that you have a solid idea of the importance of curriculum as foundation, consider how high-quality lessons can become more accessible and engaging through the principles of UDL. In this section, we will discuss how to apply the UDL principles to any curriculum and how to shift the interpretation of the definition of *fidelity*.

Curriculum fidelity is traditionally known as the extent to which teachers implement a curriculum program as intended by the developers (Bumen, Cakar, & Yildiz, 2014). Educators who use the UDL framework have to consider how to design their practice to balance implementation fidelity of the core components of a program and also how to meet the individual needs of students. Cook and Rao (2018) provide guidance on how to do this:

> We suggest that the UDL framework can provide a structure that can guide professional judgment as teachers make design decisions to adapt effective practices. The UDL guidelines are broad

enough that they can be applied to various types of instructional practices and approaches. As teachers consider a priori how to adapt a practice for their students and classroom context, they can refer to the UDL guidelines and make decisions about how to add flexibility and options to the effective practice they will use. As part of the design process (i.e., before implementing the practice), teachers can ensure that they maintain the core components of the practice and adapt it in alignment with UDL guidelines to provide multiple means of representation, expression, and engagement as appropriate for their context. The UDL guidelines can be an essential part of this instructional design process, serving as a basis for the professional judgment (p. 183).

When examining a curriculum through a UDL lens, teachers may ask: "If I were to have a truly inclusive class, and if I wanted all students to meet or exceed this standard, *and* if I were to teach this lesson, as designed, to all students, what are the possible barriers in this lesson?"

Once educators can identify possible barriers in their curriculum or lesson, the next step is to consider how to provide additional options that will allow all students to work toward the same grade-level standards. This requires a knowledge of students and available resources so that the educator can design coherent instruction.

Take a novel study in English class, for example. We reviewed a teacher's unit for the book *Speak* by Laurie Halse Anderson (2011). The publisher's website notes that every teaching unit includes a test consisting of multiple-choice questions and free-response essay writing prompts. There is absolutely nothing wrong with using a resource like this. However, we would also suggest you examine the resource through the UDL lens and supplement it with options to meet the needs of all learners. Thanks goes to our colleague Maeghan Foye for designing the following assessment in response to an analysis of *Speak*. This provides a great example of how students can work with flexible means toward firm goals while their teacher uses a more prescriptive curriculum as a foundation.

Speak is a young adult novel that follows the experiences of Melinda, a high school freshman who called the police to bust up a summer party. As a result, she is ostracized by her peers.

Maeghan had students read the book or listen to the audiobook. After reading, students had the opportunity to choose one of the following assessments. Consider how much more an assessment like the following would result in expert learning, as opposed to a traditional five-paragraph essay or a multiple-choice test.

Speak Project

Standards:

◉ Conduct short as well as more sustained research projects to answer a question (including a self-generated question) or solve a problem; narrow or broaden the inquiry when appropriate; synthesize multiple sources on the subject, demonstrating an understanding of the subject under investigation.

Given that the name of the book is *Speak*, it is unsurprising that communication versus silence is a critical theme within the book. Every character within the novel has problems with communication. Heather talks so much that she cannot hear what her friend has to say; Melinda's parents find it impossible to understand either their daughter or each other; Rachel, Melinda's former best friend, is so far removed from the protagonist that she literally begins to speak a different language. For Melinda, redemption comes through communication. Throughout the book, she explores many different methods of communicating, from passing notes to graffiti to silent protest to art. This last medium, especially, teaches her that there are many different ways to speak and use our voice.

Building on our foundation of what voice means to us in various contexts, and considering complex topics such as equality versus equity, privilege, the duty of holding space for others, and the value of taking up space ourselves, you will begin to explore the power of communication.

Potential areas to explore:

- Research a topic associated with *Speak* such as depression, anxiety, substance abuse, or another mental health concern. Create a trifold brochure or other product to inform your peers about the issue and bring awareness to our high school community. Include statistics, symptoms, help centers, and anything else that could be useful to someone struggling with their mental health. Your brochure should communicate a message of hope, support, and advocacy. You might begin with the list of resources in the back of *Speak*.

- Research a topic associated with *Speak* such as sexual assault, psychological abuse, or the characteristics of a healthy, functional romantic relationship for high school students. Create a trifold brochure or other product to inform your peers about your topic. Include statistics, symptoms, help centers, and anything else that could be useful to a teen facing one of these issues. Your brochure should communicate a message of hope, support, and advocacy. There is a list of resources in the back of *Speak*.

- Melinda is required to make her art project, a tree, come alive. Create a tree project of your own to share with the community. Your project should communicate a relevant, positive, and necessary message for your community that was influenced by research about the community. You may create a physical piece of art, such as a painting, sculpture, drawing, or collage. You may also work with media, film, or animation to create a short (3 to 5 minute), well-edited video to be shared with your peers. Your project should include a one-page artist statement that communicates your project's message and significance.

- Read the list of topics Melinda and her friends write about in their English class. Write your own essay on one of the topics. Your essay should make *arguments* that are based on a disciplinary understanding of argument and *evidence*. To support your argument, claim, or opinion well, you must include specific research related to your topic. Publish your essay and share it with our high school community.

○ Create a thoughtful, informational packet for next year's ninth graders to help them transition into high school smoothly. Research the resources available at our high school, in the local community, and within peer groups. You are encouraged to include *Speak* as one of your suggested resources. Consider what you may have liked to have known before you came to our high school. Consider what a student like Melinda may have liked to have known, as well. Your packet should be more than a survival guide; it should communicate a message of inclusivity, openness, and support.

○ Create a spoken word poem that is inspired by *Speak*. Perhaps it relates to one of the novel's main themes or symbols. Be sure to integrate research into your piece. Type and turn in a text version of your performance piece. Include a one-page, typed artist statement that communicates your poem's message and significance. Perform your poem at one of the upcoming Open Mic nights at our high school.

○ Have another idea for a project that explores the power of communication and the firm goal of the unit? Run it by me!

As you can see, providing access to an audio version of the book and developing an authentic assessment instead of using multiple-choice tests allowed Foye to provide universally designed learning experiences to all students while it also allowed her to use curriculum resources and share a reading experience with all students in her course.

The process of making a universally designed curriculum doesn't mean that teachers have to begin the process from scratch. A high-quality, off-the-shelf curriculum can be enhanced and put to good use when it is used in the context of UDL planning and implementation. Ensuring that the curriculum adoption process is well thought out and aligned to inclusive practices makes it much more likely that teachers will have a foundation with which to apply the UDL Guidelines. This maintains fidelity of core components of the program while also ensuring that all students have access to and can engage in rigorous learning experiences that meet their needs in inclusive classrooms.

A Note About Inclusion

In December 2015, Congress passed the Every Student Succeeds Act (ESSA) with bipartisan support. This law required all states to design plans to ensure that all children receive high-quality education to close achievement gaps. The ESSA legislation calls for inclusion of students with disabilities, English learners, and students from other marginalized groups to increase opportunities for success.

Inclusion placements for students with disabilities are endorsed at both the federal and state level as numerous evidence-based research studies, including a report known as the Hehir Report, commissioned by the Massachusetts Department of Elementary and Secondary Education, noted the importance of inclusion for all students with disabilities (Hehir, Grindal, & Eidelman, 2012).

Student ability was not the sole factor in these findings. Even students with severe disabilities have much higher levels of success when included with their peers. These are the key findings from the Hehir Report:

- ◑ On average, students with high-incidence disabilities who had full inclusion placements performed better than students with high-incidence disabilities who were in substantially separate placements in traditional public schools.

◒ Students with disabilities who had full inclusion placements had a higher probability of graduating high school than students with disabilities educated in substantially separate settings.

◒ Students with disabilities who had full inclusion placements were less likely to move subsequently to out-of-district placements than students educated in substantially separate settings.

It is no secret that some stakeholders reject the concept of inclusive education. But a significant amount of research supports it. Numerous peer-reviewed research studies have examined the effect of inclusion on gifted and talented students. Early studies suggested that inclusion was not effective for gifted and talented students (Brewer, Rees, & Argys, 1995). By 1999, however, research noted that inclusion was effective for gifted and talented students, but *only when* three key components were met: flexibility, acceleration, and variety (Delisle, 1999).

Flexibility provides all students with options and choices for the methods by which they learn, the materials they use to learn, and the assessments that measure their learning (which is the UDL framework). *Acceleration* allows students to move at a quicker pace if they show competency in their knowledge of the material, and *variety* allows students to personalize their learning and create meaning for themselves as they work toward standards. All three of these conditions are required in the UDL framework. Doing so will help ensure that all students have equal access to grade-level learning, equal opportunities to engage in meaningful learning, and equal expectations for their success.

Self-Reflection Questions for Leaders

1. What is your current process of curriculum adoption? Does it align to our suggested procedures? If not, how can you begin to think differently about curriculum adoption?

2. In your opinion, what is curriculum fidelity and what are the expectations of your school or district when it comes to curriculum fidelity?

3. How can a universally designed curriculum support inclusion and success for all learners, including students with disabilities, English learners, and learners who need acceleration and enrichment?

7

The Magic of Staffing

f you have been in administration for any length of time, you can look around and see the staff you brought aboard, the amazing educators who have made your school better. Hopefully you do so with pride. Chances are you also have a few of those "What was I thinking?" moments. The reason so many people laugh throughout the movie *Office Space* is because sometimes the human resources issues seem all too real.

The Appointments Clause (Article II, Section 2, Clause 2) of the United States Constitution states that the President "shall nominate and by and with the consent of the Senate, shall appoint judges of the Supreme Court." In recent years, appointments to the Supreme Court have been a source of enormous media attention given the great significance associated with the position. After all, Supreme Court justices are appointed for life. One could argue that the appointment of a Supreme Court justice is among the most important and significant actions of a sitting president. One could also argue that the hiring of staff is among the most important actions of any administrator. In many ways, hiring teachers mirrors the significance of Supreme Court appointments. Many administrators may struggle with removing a teacher who doesn't have a positive impact on learners. In business environments, if an employee does not excel, they are replaced with someone who will. In education, we don't always have that option. As with those justices, when you hire staff, you likely have them for years unless something egregious occurs. A necessary and important aspect of our job as administrators is to coach our staff members and work with them to improve. We shouldn't run education like a business because although we all demand excellence, we also need to model a growth mindset and build a culture of caring and empathy.

Coaching teachers to improve at all levels is important and rewarding work. It is also very time consuming. When the effectiveness of a given educator is low and their commitment is not 100%, coaching them can feel like a waste of resources. Coaching committed and effective educators is much more rewarding. Either way, this is a part of our position that demands more attention than it has been given in many instances. It is better to spend our time on the front end hiring those committed and effective educators rather than ones who will drag down the team.

With all the work that goes into our everyday duties, the hiring process is sometimes something we think about a couple hours before interviews (no judgment, there is *so* much else on our plates!) or when things don't quite go our way. But to transform your district, school, or department, you need to bring in the right type of educators—those who are voracious learners and critical thinkers, those who believe that all students can and will learn at high levels. If you don't put in the time to find great candidates up front, you will likely spend significantly more time trying to support new staff members.

The concept of *Person-Job fit*—that is, whether someone's skills, knowledge, and abilities match the tasks laid out in your job description—is critical in the hiring process as upfront work can ensure that you have candidates that experience both professional success and work satisfaction (Diedrich, Neubauer, & Ortner, 2018).

Person-Organization fit is equally important; that is, finding an individual whose values and beliefs align to the organization's even if their skills and competencies don't match up yet. Person-Organization fit is linked to higher job satisfaction and lower turnover. If you design a hiring process that helps identify teachers who are expert learners and champions of all students, school culture and professional learning will be a much easier process to scale.

We want to be clear that, as a leader, you should try to get both a Person-Job fit *and* a Person-Organization fit, and that doing so is worth your time and effort in the long run. You want a skills match (Person-Job) and also a beliefs and values match (Person-Organization). So, let's start the hiring process from the beginning. You have posted the job, reviewed the resumes, selected applicants, and created an interview committee. It's tempting to google "Best interview questions" and hope for the best, but the structure of an interview and the types of questions you ask really matter.

Using questions that are based on job analysis, taking notes during the interview, using a panel of interviewers, and using rating scales to evaluate the interviewees' answers make an interview more effective (Pulakos & Schmitt, 1995). Like planning a UDL lesson, the key to hiring success comes from proactively designing the interview process. Doing so will allow the interview team to identify an all-star teacher about whom you will someday brag and say, "I was on the hiring team for her."

We have created the following screening protocol that you can use or adapt to find a great candidate for your school or district. Additionally, we have provided some sample questions that may get you thinking about what you may want to ask after completing the screening process.

Interview Committee Protocol

This process typically requires a substantial shift in thinking from analyzing the activities included in the job description (what a person does) to identifying the major job results (what the new hire will be expected to deliver).

1. All interview committee members review the job description for the vacant position.

2. All committee members consider the following question: If this person does all the activities in the job description, what are we expecting this person to accomplish and deliver? Think here about "firm goals, flexible means."

3. Each committee member writes their individual expectations on a Post-it or online collaboration tool like Padlet or Google Jamboard (one expectation on each Post-it) and the facilitator thematically codes results. These expectations will include the knowledge, skills, and behavioral characteristics (KSBCs) that would be necessary for the candidate to successfully achieve the job results.

   ● **Knowledge:** What formalized training, education, or prior job experience is necessary for the candidate to be successful (i.e., knowledge of inclusive practice, dual certified in special education, trained in antiracism)?

   ● **Skills:** What proficiencies would the candidate need to be successful? For example, the candidate could have the appropriate license and education, but are they an effective communicator (i.e., responds to feedback effectively, adept at using instructional technology)?

   ● **Behavioral characteristics:** How would a successful employee consistently act within the culture? Look back to your core values in this step!

4. After identifying themes, participants will collaborate in groups of three to four to prioritize KSBCs using the

following coding. You can encourage groups to write their lists on chart paper, on individual Post-its, or on something similar.

- ◕ Priority level 1 means KSBCs that they must bring to the job on the first day.

- ◕ Priority level 2 means they can develop these on the job and that the organization has the time and resources to accomplish this training.

- ◕ Priority level 3 means these KSBCs are preferred but not necessary.

5. Each group then identifies their Priority 1 KSBCs to share with the group. The facilitator discusses themes and commonalities and helps the group narrow down the list to the four to six KSBCs that are most critical for job success.

6. Once you have four to six KSBCs, draft interview questions that will help the committee determine if the candidate meets the requirements. Table 7.1 is an example of how the list of Priority 1 KSBCs is aligned to interview questions. Reflect on how the answers to the questions would allow the interview committee to determine if the person is the best fit.

7. During the interview, when questions are asked, everyone on the interview committee can rank the answers using the following scale so you can create a comprehensive rating scale and a strong foundation you can use to discuss the candidates.

- ◕ Three points: The answer was thoughtful, comprehensive, and complex. Candidate clearly possesses the KSBC and would be able to bring it to the job on Day 1.

● Two points: The candidate answered the question partially; they may have the KSBC based on their answer, but something was clearly missing.

● One point: The answer missed the mark, was concerning, or otherwise did not reflect that the candidate possesses the KSBC.

Table 7.1: Designing Interview Questions to Align to KSBCs

KSBC	Corresponding Interview Questions
Believes "all means all"	★ In our district, we believe that when students don't learn, it's because teaching, curriculum, and the school need to be designed differently. How do you feel about that statement?
Experience teaching in an inclusive setting (i.e., prior position, student teaching)	★ How do you go about preparing for a lesson/unit to ensure that the needs of all students are met through options and choices? ★ If I were to walk into your classroom, what would I see? Describe the environment and how the lesson would be proactively designed to meet the needs of all learners. ★ How do you engage learners who may face barriers in rigorous, meaningful learning experiences?
Learner-centered	★ How would you use student feedback to improve your instruction and ensure that you are developing authentic choices and options to improve their learning?
Evidence-informed	★ Tell us about assessments you use to inform instruction and how you utilize the results of these assessments in your practice.
Skilled at educational technology	★ How would you use technology to enhance your instruction and provide students with multiple ways to access information or express their understanding?

KSBC	Corresponding Interview Questions
Reflective expert learner	★ Tell us about two different lessons—one that you expected would go well, and it did; and another you expected to go well, and it didn't. What was different about the design of the two lessons?
Strong collaborator with all stakeholders	★ We encourage and promote collaboration and professionalism in our school. Give us an example from your experiences of how you have worked collaboratively with colleagues, parents, and/or students to design learning experiences that meet the needs of all learners. ★ How will you handle home/school communication to ensure that you develop meaningful communication with all families, regardless of variability?

One important consideration is looking for and hiring teachers who are likely to align their practices to the UDL framework (Person-Job fit) and who believe that students need different options and choices to meet their greatest potential (Person-Organization fit). To make this possible, hiring practices need to result in the most qualified candidates. Typical procedures include interview questions, as we just shared, but we argue you can use more meaningful ways to determine if an educator is a great fit for your community after a candidate has been selected as a finalist based on their interview. These include demonstration lessons and writing prompts.

Demo Lesson Protocol

Think of an interview as a first step in your onboarding process. Ideally, however, you would have an opportunity to see a teacher interact with students and teach a lesson. You can adapt or use the following demo lesson protocol to ensure that teachers you are considering have a strong background in UDL, or you can use it to provide your candidate with feedback about your expectations for curriculum design moving forward, if they do get the job.

If you do not have students in session when you are interviewing, you may adapt this protocol to include a lesson plan review so that you are familiar with the teacher's design process and whether they proactively address barriers that would prevent learning at high levels.

1. After a successful first interview, email the candidate and invite them for a second interview, the focus of which will be a demonstration lesson. Ensure that you share the school's commitment to UDL and provide them with options and choices for how to design the lesson. For example, you may write the following:

   We'd like to invite you back for a second interview, which will include a 15-to-20-minute demonstration lesson in _____ [provide grade/course title]. As you may have seen in the job posting, the district is committed to inclusive practices and Universal Design for Learning (UDL), so you will need to plan for an inclusive classroom with diverse students. If you need some background in UDL, or if you want to view an exemplar lesson, please review one or more of the following resources [insert links to articles, videos, etc.].

   You may choose any topic that aligns to the standards for your position. Please bring a lesson plan, using any format you wish, or use the district template [insert district template if there is one]. We will discuss your lesson at the pre-demonstration conference.

2. When the candidate arrives for the second interview, spend 10 minutes reviewing the prepared lesson plan. Ask questions about their design process and how they

integrated what they learned about UDL into the design process.

3. Observe the lesson and take notes as you would as a component of your teacher evaluation process.

4. After the lesson, proceed to the post-demonstration interview. During this session, ask the candidate to reflect on the effectiveness of the lesson and provide mastery-oriented feedback and praise where it is due. You may want to use any of the following prompts to scaffold the reflection process:

   a. Do you feel that the students were engaged in your lesson? How do you know?

   b. Did all students achieve your objectives?

   c. Were there any barriers that you had not anticipated? Describe what happened.

   d. How would you design the lesson differently if you were to teach it again?

Sample "Writing" Prompts

Another option is to use sample "writing" prompts to explore a candidate's knowledge of content and pedagogy. As with all things UDL, think about the true goal of the exercise and then remove the barriers. When candidates arrive for the interview, provide three possible prompts, like the ones that follow. Provide them with graphic organizers, a Google suite of tools (including voice to text), and a computer. Provide them with the option to use voice recording or video if they are more comfortable with those formats. Encourage them to come as early as necessary to complete the prompt, sharing the expectation that it should only be one to two pages. You could even provide a rubric with how you will assess the prompt and provide an exemplar. Just as it is critical to make learning accessible to students, the same must be provided to teachers.

- ⮑ You have a classroom of students of varied developmental levels and concept understanding. Describe which instructional strategies you would use in a typical lesson to ensure that you meet the needs of all learners.
- ⮑ Prepare a letter/video to the families of your students describing the objectives of an upcoming lesson and how you will move all students to intended learning goals.
- ⮑ Describe how you will use data from assessments to inform classroom instruction so it meets the needs of all learners.

After the writing prompt, proceed to the interview. During the interview, ask the candidate to reflect on their response. You may ask: "How do you feel about the response you wrote?"

Supporting Teachers in UDL From the Beginning

Once we have the right person on board, we have some other considerations. Many new teachers are not coming to our schools with a wealth of knowledge about UDL. Even if you have already done extensive work with providing your current staff with UDL-centered professional development (PD), your new teachers are going to need some PD on UDL.

The first step is to make sure you match them up with a strong mentor who has experience in UDL. Next, you will need to provide exposure to UDL practices to your new staff. Encourage and nurture a climate of peer observations with them. Work to get them in classrooms where UDL practices are successful. One of the best things about being an administrator is you have the opportunity to be in so many classes every week. When you visit classrooms, you may realize quickly how many tremendous teachers you have in your school or district. But it is important that you get these amazing teachers out of isolation. We learn best from each other. Get your new staff in classrooms with the best teachers and good things will happen. You may also want to consider some type of UDL online modules for new staff.

Ten Quick and Dirty Tips for Supporting Teachers in UDL From the Beginning

Consider the following list of strategies that you can implement to ensure that you are supporting the best candidates so they will have both professional success, job embedded support, and most importantly, job satisfaction!

1. Assign each new teacher a mentor who is skilled in UDL lesson planning, and be sure the new hire has time to observe the mentor in action.

2. Create a Google document folder, or Padlet, with UDL lesson ideas shared by teachers in your school. Consider sharing resources like Goalbook's list of UDL-aligned strategies. There are hundreds of them at https://goalbookapp.com/toolkit/v/strategies.

3. Create a monthly or quarterly newsletter on best practices that includes resources from your district and others.

4. Instill confidence that taking risks is not only okay but encouraged. Maybe even hand out a risk pass so new staff members know they can take a risk on lesson design.

5. Suggest professional learning goals for new teachers to help them focus on UDL implementation. Providing a list of possible goals is a great strategy for helping them align their practice to the expectations of the school or district.

6. Create opportunities for peer observations—and provide substitute coverage yourself if you have to!

7. Be excited when you see UDL in their practice. Make sure to have a face-to-face meeting to share your appreciation of their efforts, or share a quick email, drop a thank-you card off, or bring them a treat like a gift card for a coffee.

8. Have UDL publications like *UDL Now*, *Equity by Design*, and *Innovate Inside the Box* available in staff workrooms, at the lunch table, and in other common places so they have access to professional development at their fingertips.

9. Model UDL in how you design your faculty meetings and professional development offerings so they can experience the power of having multiple means of representation, action and expression, and engagement.

10. Be visible. Drop in for informal observations, provide feedback, offer to model lessons. Remember how difficult it was to start a new position, and do whatever you can to foster collaboration, community, and culture.

If we are to truly transform our classrooms, schools, and districts, we need the right people working with our students. Because staffing is one of our most important tasks, it's critical that we design onboarding procedures so we can determine how to find the candidates that are both "good at it"—and will be likely to have professional success—and "happy with it"—which means they will be satisfied with the work in an inclusive, universally designed learning environment (Diedrich, Neubauer, & Ortner, 2018).

In preparation for your next vacancy, consider the following next steps. Choose one or more that will work best for you and your team.

◑ Review your interview protocols and process. If you don't have opportunities for members of the interview committee to reflect on critical knowledge, skills, and behavioral characteristics that are necessary for new hires, share our proposed process at a faculty meeting, at a parent advisory group, or in some other forum so you can begin to discuss a transition to a more comprehensive process.

- Review the list of "Ten Quick and Dirty Tips" for supporting new hires in UDL. Be honest with yourself about how many you implement. Set a goal to incorporate one additional strategy into your practice this month.

- Check out the list of UDL strategies at Goalbook and share your takeaways with your staff so they can see your commitment to ongoing, expert learning in your own practice. See https://goalbookapp.com/toolkit/v/strategies to learn more.

Self-Reflection Questions for Leaders

1. How can interview questions help you to find candidates that have the necessary knowledge, skills, and behavioral characteristics to meet the needs of all students in inclusive settings?

2. How can you improve your hiring practices to ensure you have the best candidates to implement UDL?

3. Once you hire new staff members, how can you incorporate universally designed support to ensure successful onboarding?

8

A Schedule That Supports UDL Within a Multitiered System

Every school must create a schedule that can work for their students, teachers, and communities. In a universally designed school, we don't just want lessons to be flexible. The whole school environment needs to be flexible as well. Traditional schedules and block schedules are designed in a factory model. A bell rings, and everyone moves. Not the best model for expert learning.

It is clear that due to the growing diversity of school populations, universally designed schedules permit extended learning time for those students who need additional time to meet course expectations, or for students to get enrichment. Having time to provide students with what they need, whether intervention or enrichment, in addition to rigorous Tier 1 course offerings is critical when building an effective multitiered system of support (MTSS) that meets the needs of all students. If we want all learners to have access to Tier 1, we also have to ensure they have access to any additional support or specially designed instruction that is necessary.

A schedule can be one of the biggest technical barriers standing in our way of meeting the needs of students and staff. A fundamental truth in education is that there is no perfect schedule. No matter how you attack it, there will be holes. Prioritizing what is most important in a schedule and aligning it with your core values can help to identify what changes you need to make. As we stated in the introduction, fear of change is a real thing. Changing or even modifying a schedule can be a monumental task and is one that many administrators will gladly put off unless it is absolutely necessary. Remember, though, that putting off that difficult conversation or saying "I will start exercising and taking care of myself next week, next month, or next year" is just going to make things more difficult in the short term. Once a schedule is in a place that will allow flexibility, you will be so much more able to implement real change and adapt to the needs of all students.

Teachers could plan UDL lessons in isolation without collaborating with others. That is possible, but it is not ideal. As we would expect students to build their skills through collaboration, so too should we expect that of our staff. Sometimes the complexity of the schedule can severely hinder our ability to make staff collaboration possible on a daily or weekly basis. When schedules are built to accommodate the principles of UDL, teachers will have the ability to collaborate with other teachers on a regular basis. Sharing insights, successes, and failures with our colleagues is essential to increasing the frequency of UDL-driven lessons in our schools. As you think about your teacher schedules, reflect on and discuss the following questions:

- ➲ Do you have sufficient time for shared planning?
- ➲ If there is common planning, what types of activities occur during these meetings?
- ➲ How is common planning time supported to ensure it is implemented well and rigorously?

To help define *sufficient time*, consider the following guidance adapted from *Learning Time: In Pursuit of Educational Equity* (Saunders, de Velasco, & Oakes, 2017). Check whether your school schedule presently allows for each of the following:

- Sixty min/week for grade-level meetings (minimum)
- Sixty min/week for data analysis (minimum)
- Opportunities for regular content-level team meetings
- Partner staff to regularly participate in teacher meetings discussing student progress
- Student support services staff to regularly participate in teacher meetings discussing student progress
- Specialty/elective teachers to regularly participate in teacher meetings discussing student progress
- Opportunities for additional informal/non-mandatory grade-level meetings during common planning/prep time
- Opportunities for additional informal/non-mandatory content-level meetings during common planning/ prep time
- Additional collaboration time beyond regularly scheduled meetings, such as peer observations, coaching, full faculty PD, and so on

If the answer to these prompts is "yes," you're in good shape for teacher common planning time. If many of your answers are "not yet," consider creating action plans around schedule adoption that would allow for such critical professional activities.

ERS (2018) offers some concrete ways to revise an existing schedule to ensure more common planning time. Their suggestions include stacking two blocks of planning time together, reducing planning time on a few days to increase time on another day, reorganizing time that teachers have at the beginning and end of the day into more team planning time, scheduling noninstructional blocks like recess and lunch next to planning time, creating larger specials classes so that you can cover more core teachers' time with fewer such classes, and creating WIN (What I Need) blocks.

The National Council for Learning Disabilities and Understood (2019) offer additional tips for finding common planning time. They encourage leaders to look into scheduling regular (e.g., weekly/monthly) early dismissal or late-start days for teacher collaboration and to create communication systems so that faculty meetings do not have to be used for "housekeeping" items.

We also must allow student interests and needs to drive schedule construction. For example, in Mike's high school, heavy emphasis is placed on student choice in determining what elective offerings will run from year to year. Students help create new courses and advocate for opportunities outside of school to access real-world experiences. Students can take classes at local colleges and receive credit. Student internships provide insight into possible future career paths. The COVID pandemic made some of these community opportunities more difficult to access, but students, when driven by their interests, were very creative in identifying other opportunities that were able to fit within district safety protocols. Having a schedule that allows students to participate in these real-world experiences is critical at all levels.

A universally designed schedule dedicates time for intervention and/or enrichment blocks for all students. For students in need of additional support in a targeted area, the intervention block provides an opportunity for students to choose to review, relearn, and master the skills in that area. For students who have demonstrated proficiency in the curriculum being taught in their classrooms, or who need an additional level of challenge, the enrichment block provides an option for students to develop a deeper understanding of key concepts and to apply and integrate learning from core content.

Enrichment opportunities may also include such options as independent study, virtual coursework, a service-learning program, or entrepreneurship opportunities. Essentially, the school designs a schedule that provides every student with what they need so students get a block of time—let's say 45 minutes—every day in which they can self-reflect and choose learning experiences that work best for them. In an elementary school, some students may work with a reading specialist for intervention while a classmate participates in Reader's Theater for fluency. Still other classmates may work on coding video games with a technology integration specialist.

A UDL-informed schedule must focus on identifying ways in which students can access Tier 2 or Tier 3 intervention opportunities without being pulled from existing classes. One way schools can address this in their existing schedules is to add an additional block on a daily or weekly basis. An intervention block could allow students to meet with staff members regularly to address difficulties they may be having in a given subject, or this time could also be used and promoted to provide enrichment to students who wish to push themselves past the existing curriculum in a given subject, for clubs and activities, for information needs, and more. There doesn't have to be a single purpose for this set-aside time, but it is essential that we make this time available within the school day for those who need it.

When the three UDL principles are implemented, we can create classrooms that are truly inclusive and can meet the variable needs of all students. Often, educators may struggle with this concept of inclusion because so many of our models are deficit-based and focus on the skills that students don't have. We understand that in our world, students have varying levels of needs and sometimes our classrooms, however universally designed and inclusive they are, will not offer enough to close the gap for students who need it most.

Whether our students struggle academically, behaviorally, socially, and/or emotionally, they all deserve a universally designed education just because they showed up in the morning.

Sometimes, however, we need to supplement this universally designed Tier 1 instruction with intervention or enrichment. Individual education plans (IEPs) can help provide additional support in order to meet students' very unique needs. When we think about inclusive classrooms, the sticking point is usually how we can possibly give students all the services they need in the general education classroom.

First, we cannot emphasize enough that all students need access to inclusive classrooms. We discussed this previously, but it begs repeating. A report published by the National Council on Disabilities (2018) sums up the research on inclusion: "[W]hen students are included, they have more access to the general curriculum and effective instruction, they achieve at higher rates of academic performance, and they acquire better social and behavioral outcomes" (p. 37). Additionally, the report notes that students without disabilities made comparable or greater gains academically when taught in general education classes with students who had learning disabilities while they also experienced reduced fear of human differences, increased comfort and awareness of differences, growth in social cognition, improvements in self-concept, growth of ethical principles, and caring friendships. (If you are interested in more research on inclusion, we highly recommend reading the full report, which is titled "IDEA Series: The Segregation of Students With Disabilities.")

When you start to think about reading services, adjustment counseling, speech and language services, and English language services, you may wonder how to deliver these *and* high-quality Tier 1 instruction with your current staff levels. This is why we urge you to think differently about scheduling. In particular, we endorse the concept of creating a schedule that has an additional block a day where no Tier 1 instruction happens. We call this block the WIN block for "What I Need." Some districts call it a flex block, an extension block, an intervention block, or a plus block. Regardless of its name, setting aside this time is critical to maximize universally designed instruction.

Creating a schedule that has additional time is not without barriers itself. Clearly, there are only so many minutes in a day, and if you're going to add an additional block, you're going to have to take minutes from somewhere else. We understand that class time is precious, but the class time that remains in Tier 1 is maximized when every student truly has an opportunity to be challenged and supported in ways that are linguistically and culturally responsive.

We cannot stress enough the importance of working with teachers throughout this process. In our district, we instituted the WIN block at levels K–8 before we transitioned to looking at a new schedule for the high school. As a first step at the high school, we met with all academic advisors, who are similar to department heads in some other districts, to let them know that we were looking to move in that direction. We also had a staff meeting and ran an activity that we called "Minute to Win It." We asked everyone to imagine they were in charge of creating a schedule for the school with the WIN block. We asked them to consider how long it would be, how often it would meet, where students would go, and what students would do during that time. They then had to share their best ideas in the minute presentation. As a next step, we sent out a survey to all curriculum leaders asking the following questions:

- Primarily, what would you use a WIN block for?
- What would be the biggest advantage to having a WIN block?
- What is the biggest obstacle in establishing a WIN block?
- How many days a week should we have a WIN block?
- What should the duration of a WIN block be?
- How soon should we pilot our WIN block?

We offered space for our department leaders to share their own thoughts about the initiative that may not have been included in the survey. We wanted to gain a sense of how differently representatives from all departments viewed the addition of a WIN block—the concerns and priorities that would affect our efforts to implement a schedule that worked for all learners. Curriculum leaders were asked to share the results of our survey with departments to gather feedback for next steps.

Schedule Adoption Tips

- If you're not able to make your school day longer through collective bargaining, you will have to evaluate your schedule and take something away. Whether your school has a traditional schedule or a block schedule, consider decreasing each class in order to incorporate a WIN block.

- Before beginning, identify the problem areas in your master schedules; develop and implement modified schedules; monitor their impact; and refine, revise, or redevelop a new schedule, as necessary.

- Collaborate with your educators and find innovative ways to increase buy-in. For example, you may consider offering advisory twice a month during the WIN block or offering an "exploratory" day where students can try an elective they wouldn't otherwise be able to fit in their schedule.

- When designing the schedule, use achievement and performance data to schedule students to receive tiered support when needed, and allow for the movement of students between tiers when appropriate. Students who need targeted intervention also need options to access enrichment opportunities.

Schedule Considerations

No schedule is perfect, but a number of models provide examples for how to schedule Tier 2 and Tier 3 intervention in addition to providing all students with access to Tier 1 instruction. Keep in mind that these are only examples; it may take a few years to develop an ideal schedule for your school. All schedules need to be reviewed annually and revised as needed.

Elementary Considerations

Although you can approach creating a schedule that supports a tiered system of instruction in different ways, the first step should be to determine which model will best suit your school and staff. When examining the WIN blocks at the elementary level, consider which approach would be more advantageous to your school.

Regrouping Approach: In this model, all of the classes in each grade level are combined for the intervention and enrichment blocks, allowing for a more discrete grouping of students and a more varied range of enrichment opportunities. The students move to different locations around the school and receive intervention/support or enrichment services from the most qualified school personnel including their classroom teachers.

Centers Approach: In this approach, all students receive intervention/enrichment within their own classroom. Transition time is eliminated, which allows for more time to be spent on learning, and students are able to stay focused and are less distracted. This model encourages teachers to share instructional practices and allows for services for students with disabilities to be provided within the general education environment.

Secondary Considerations

The following are sample schedules that incorporate a block for intervention and enrichment (i.e., a WIN block) at the secondary level. Enrichment opportunities at the secondary level may include such options as independent study, virtual coursework, a service-learning program, or entrepreneurship opportunities.

You will note that schedules have slightly different blocks of time for the WIN block. This is because research provides no agreement about a definitive amount of time being necessary to provide intervention. All sample schedules, however, fall within ranges recommended in the *Self-Study Guide for Implementing High School Academic Interventions*, published by the Institute for Education Sciences (Smith et al., 2016).

Sample 1: Block Schedule With Four Lunches

In Sample 1, the WIN block occurs every day for 31 minutes. Courses had to be decreased from 86 minutes to 78 minutes to ensure the time for the WIN block. C block has a rotating lunch, so some students may begin C block, break for lunch, and complete C block after lunch.

A Block	7:27–8:45 (78 minutes)
WIN Block	8:49–9:20 (31 minutes)
B Block	9:24–10:42 (78 minutes)
C Block	10:46–12:28 (78 minutes + 24 min for rotating lunch)
D Block	12:32–1:50 (78 minutes)

Sample 2: Block Schedule With Two Lunches

In Sample 2, the WIN block occurs every day for 40 minutes, opposite a 25-minute lunch. While the first group has lunch, half the staff offers WIN support; then the schedule switches. This model would be more ideal for small schools that can serve all students in two lunches.

A Block	7:35–8:52 (77 Min)	
B Block	8:56–10:13 (77 Min)	
C Block	10:18–11:35 (77 Min)	
	Group 1	Group 2
Lunch/WIN	11:42–12:08 (25 Min) Lunch	11:42–12:23 (40 Min)
WIN/Lunch	12:12–12:52 (40 Min)	12:28–12:53 (25 Min)
D Block	12:58–2:15 (77 Min)	

Sample 3: Traditional Schedule

Similar to Sample 2, in Sample 3, the WIN block occurs every day for 40 minutes, opposite a 25-minute lunch. Given that this is a traditional schedule, providing students with seven (7) periods a day, classes had to be reduced from 43 minutes to 40 minutes each.

Period 1	7:30–8:10 (40 Min)	
Period 2	8:13–8:53 (40 Min)	
Period 3	8:56–9:36 (40 Min)	
Period 4	9:39–10:19 (40 Min)	
Period 5	10:22–11:02 (40 Min)	
Period 6	11:05–11:45 (40 Min)	
	Group 1	Group 2
Lunch/WIN	11:42–12:07 (25 Min)	11:42–12:22 (40 Min)
WIN/Lunch	12:10–12:50 (40 Min)	12:25–12:50 (25 Min)
Period 7	12:53–1:33 (40 Min)	

Sample 4: Middle School Schedule

Sample 4 is unique to middle school, as lower grades may still offer recess and that needs to be built into a master schedule. In this model, the WIN Block is 40 minutes in grades 5–6 and increases to 50 minutes in grades 7–8. Given that this is a traditional schedule with seven (7) periods a day, classes were reduced from 58 minutes to 50 minutes each. Integrated arts (IA) courses can be scheduled and switched each quarter or semester to offer students multiple experiences that will help to provide a holistic schedule that meets their needs.

Period	Length	Time	Grade 5	Grade 6	Grade 7	Grade 8
Period 1	50 min	8:08–8:58	CORE	CORE	IA	CORE
Period 2	50 min	8:58–9:48	CORE	CORE	CORE	IA
Period 3	50 min	9:48–10:38	IA	IA	CORE	CORE
Period 4/ Lunch	77 min	10:38–11:55	Recess (10:38–10:50)	Recess (10:38–10:50)	WIN (50 min) (10:38–11:28)	WIN (50 min) (10:38–11:28)
			Lunch (10:50–11:15)	Lunch (10:50–11:15)		
			WIN (40 min) (11:15–11:55)	WIN (40 min) (11:15–11:55)	Lunch (11:28–11:55)	Lunch (11:28–11:55)
Period 5	50 min	11:55–12:45	CORE	CORE	IA	IA
Period 6	50 min	12:45–1:35	CORE	IA	CORE	CORE
Period 7	50 min	1:35–2:25	IA	CORE	CORE	CORE

In our research for incorporating a flex or WIN block, we talked with a number of schools in various stages of WIN block implementation. No surprise here . . . it is an adjustment for staff with numerous bumps in the road. We would love to tell you exactly how to seamlessly incorporate this into your schedule, but like most other things, it depends on the unique barriers you face. Possible barriers include a struggle to get buy-in from staff on the usefulness or effectiveness of the new model, working with the union to negotiate changes in daily expectations, teacher preparedness to run an effective WIN block, and finding a manageable system to get students in the right spot each day so that everyone is accounted for at all times.

These are real obstacles to get over and it may take some time. The administrators we spoke with, however, unanimously stressed that although there were bumps in the road in terms of implementation, they were fully convinced that adding the WIN block was what was best for their students.

Administrators shared that being able to provide enrichment activities, especially in elementary and middle school, really added some value to students' school days because it gave them some choice time that they hadn't had before. Overwhelmingly, the aspect of additional interventions for students was the number one positive takeaway.

Open Honors: A High School Pilot

Many high school schedules are built on a system in which students are leveled into certain courses as they reach or approach high school. These rigid "tracks" are sometimes barriers that prevent students from accessing advanced coursework or taking courses that are most interesting to them. Once the leveling begins, it is very hard to reverse. Many districts have initiated efforts to reduce leveling at the high school level.

To do this you will need to, once again, approach teachers and teacher leaders who are expert learners and willing to say yes to change. Sometimes we almost cringe just getting the words out: "What would you think about running three grade levels of English in one section?" or "How about we put all levels of students in your grade 9 history class and offer 'open honors'?" Although we may hesitate to ask, it is essential that we do so. Buy-in is critical, and these teachers can help you get more comprehensive support from your staff.

Open honors can be embedded in inclusive classrooms. In this model, all students take a class together, but students who choose to take the class for honors complete more comprehensive assignments. This is a great example of finding ways "within" your existing schedule to get high quality, rigorous instruction to all students when you are not able to make or not ready for a large-scale change to your daily schedule.

UDL is implemented at high levels in our 9th grade English/language arts department. Because of their strong background in UDL, the teachers in this department volunteered to pilot the change. They were able to design curriculum that not only met the needs of a variety of learners, but also provided students with the option of self-assessing their own learning. If you'd like to explore the open honors concept in your current secondary schedule, the following guidance may support your first steps.

Strategies for Getting Started on Open/Embedded Honors (From Potter, 2019)

○ **Start conversations about the value of diverse classrooms.** Getting buy-in from teachers is essential. Create time for staff conversations about any concerns that may arise from the transition. Lead educators to reflect on how ability grouping influenced their own educations (and those of their peers) growing up. Ask teachers to share examples of how students with different academic abilities have benefited each other in the classroom. If possible, facilitate visits at other schools that use embedded honors models.

○ **Identify planning time for teachers.** The biggest resource needed to implement open/embedded honors is teacher planning time. School administrators and department leads should examine how to rearrange planning schedules so that teachers can have the planning time they need to implement the program well. Teachers may also use collective bargaining as a tool to help secure planning time for open honors.

○ **Start with one team or department.** Schools can try out open honors by starting with just one class or subject. If schools are starting from a position of having de-tracked classes, adding an open honors component to several classes could begin with just a few short meetings (on curriculum development and ways to enroll students).

Making whole-scale schedule changes may be the best way to address large barriers to meeting the needs of all of our students. If you have ever participated in a large-scale schedule change, you know that this is a difficult and time-consuming process. If the genesis of this change isn't coming from staff, you will certainly have an uphill road ahead of you.

If you are in a position to make a large-scale shift in the schedule, it may be the best long-term solution ahead of you. If you would like to see change but are not in a position to make a large-scale schedule change, you will need to be creative in making changes within your schedule.

Rest assured, we understand that for many, creating a more flexible schedule will be a difficult task, but sooner or later you may need to make changes. It doesn't hurt to identify what will need to be done, even if it is something for the future. The following steps may help you begin your journey toward addressing barriers in your own schedule:

- Research your state guidance on multitiered systems of support that require that all students access Tier 1 instruction while also receiving supplemental support. Share the guidance with staff while also sharing your current schedule. Encourage staff to identify barriers in the schedule.

- Consider bringing together a group of stakeholders for a scheduling committee. Even if you don't make changes to your schedule, it's beneficial to review it in light of current research on inclusion to determine if changes are needed.

- Contact administrators in your area to identify schools that are implementing a WIN block, a flex block, or something similar. Ask if you can observe the practice of such a block during the period, talk to teachers, and/or bring staff to visit to experience the power of supplemental support as opposed to supplanted support.

- Review the inclusion rates of schools in your area. Identify the schools that are most inclusive and schedule a chat or coffee with the school leaders to see how they were able to eliminate barriers that often prevent inclusion.

Self-Reflection Questions for Leaders

1. Are all of your students currently enrolled in inclusive general education classrooms that are universally designed? If they are not, what barriers prevent all students from being educated together?

2. What are the strengths and barriers in your current schedule and how can the guidance in this chapter help you to build a better schedule to meet the needs of all students?

3. How can you begin to have difficult conversations about ability grouping with your staff as the educational research begins to push more schools toward scheduling decisions like implementing open honors?

9

Conclusion

When students enter school at the primary levels, they are given so many opportunities to be perseverant. Usually they are assessed on standards-based report cards, which push students to keep going, using terms like *emerging*, *progressing*, or *nearing mastery* of the standard. When working with our youngest learners, we discuss learning as a journey, embrace a growth mindset, and remind them about the power of "yet."

By the time they leave high school, in most cases, they have been assessed by letter grades that label them and rank them. Learning has become something they are good at, or not good at. We are not casting blame on schools. The system is set up for this type of rating and ranking. Colleges and universities across the country would like a clear indicator of where students are compared to their peers. How do they rank? What are their standardized test scores, GPAs, and similar metrics? This is changing in some places, but the movement is slow and incremental.

All of this can thwart students' growth, perseverance, and risk-taking. And in many ways, that model has seeped into leadership—the focus is on strong leadership and weak leadership that does not recognize the continuum of growth that is possible for all of us. Instead, we need a universally designed system that values expert learning, continuous improvement, and evidence-based decision-making. To implement this, we have to deconstruct our traditional systems.

We want to end this book with a reminder of how poorly designed learning environments can create inequities and exclude many learners. As a parent, Mike has seen the way one-size-fits-all teaching affected his daughter. After receiving a C on a test, his daughter took the initiative to meet virtually with her teacher during office hours. She explained that she was struggling in her approach, that she had studied very hard, done all the work, and thought she was ready, only to bomb the most recent test. She asked for support and said she was willing to show what she learned in a different way or retake the test after additional support. She learned quickly, however, that the teacher's philosophy mirrored the traditional system.

"I don't give retakes," the teacher explained.

"Well, how about some extra credit or an alternative assessment?" she asked. The reply was, "I don't do that either."

As Mike listened to the conversation from the other room, he heard a young woman, one who had done a great job being proactive and confident, get completely shut down. She was told if she wanted better grades, she would simply have to do better on the tests.

This is an example of a classroom that is one-size-fits-all and inflexible. Those students who flourish under that particular class's instruction, engagement strategies, and assessments will do well, and that will be reflected on their transcripts. Those students who need more support, alternative pathways, or more flexibility may fail. This has to change. And you can change it.

As you grow in your practice as an expert learner and a leader in a universally designed school or district, you have to embrace perseverance, the importance of growth mindset, and the value of consistent reflection and change. Like elementary students, it is critical that you think of your practice as emerging if you are just beginning and know that there is always room for improvement. You can always try again, take an alternative path, and continue to grow. There is no ceiling, no 100%, no A+ on being a leader. Expert learning and leading is a lifetime commitment and cannot flourish in a traditional system.

In our introduction we emphasized the importance and difficulty of change. Changes in our lives and in our profession are challenging but eventually we need to make the choice to take the risk because the reward is too great and our students' education is too important.

We also talked about our love for Coelho's *The Alchemist*. We would like to share one more nugget of wisdom from the text. The author describes the anguish that Santiago felt when he made the choice to leave all that he had known to pursue his treasure: "He had to choose between something he had become accustomed to and something he wanted to have." This is where so many school and district leaders as well as teachers are right now. Will we have the courage to take the risk in order to begin the greater work we are called to do? The answer, of course, is yes, or you would have stopped reading long ago.

Committing to the UDL framework will require us to change our beliefs, our skills, and our system so we have a positive impact on all learners, especially those learners who have been historically marginalized and minoritized. This is our most important work. Yes, we know we are all busy. But despite the whirlwind, our work is about equity and inclusion and equal opportunities to learn.

A study by the U.S. Department of Education's Institute for Education Sciences chronicles some of the hours and tasks of typical principals (Lavigne et al., 2016). Most are working 60+ hours per week. We know that district administrators are in the same boat. Many of you are likely doing more than that. You are likely exhausted, and this may be another thing, and it feels like it might be the one that breaks the camel's back. But it is not.

Regardless of where you are in your leadership practice, take the time, and take the risk, and focus on UDL. Now. The reality is that risk-taking can feel scary. But expert leaders are willing to launch from comfort to take risks. And when you model this leadership and this vulnerability, your colleagues, students, and families will notice. We know this to be true because we have lived it.

At first, it may feel like you are beginning the initiative, and the changes, alone. And you will come up against educators who do not believe in retakes, or flexible pathways. But you have to continue to focus on what's wildly important. Commit to being an expert learner and start with core values, modeling, and high-quality professional learning, and soon, you will have colleagues by your side, willing to join you in this critical work. Equity and inclusion require collaboration.

One of our colleagues, Jon O'Connor, who is a digital arts and photography teacher, said it best. After five years of UDL implementation, he wanted to send a note to new teachers in a newsletter we prepare for educators in our mentoring program. Although we have both made many missteps and many, many mistakes, we also have incredible moments when we can stop, for just a second, and celebrate. Having a colleague who wanted to share the power and promise of UDL with new staff was one of those celebrations. Jon penned the following. We want to end the book with his words:

> *Save time and tears: Take a risk and target UDL. Give yourself permission to put the oxygen mask on yourself first. Most teachers aren't lazy, quite the opposite! The term "teacher burnout" is an unfair one since it implies the teacher simply fizzled out for lack of emotional or mental reserve. As a teacher I simply want to make steady systematic change and am wary of any drastic overhauls that may prove to be short lived. But the profession is increasingly complex and knowing where to invest effort and where to avoid wasted energy is critical to maintaining sanity. C'mon—take a risk and try UDL. It will reduce wasted effort (time) and reduce wasted emotional*

energy (tears). This is especially true, I would argue, for those who have been avoiding implementing UDL out of exhaustion. Our task is to create an environment that encourages risk-taking and shares ownership with our students. As with all effective universal design, this begins with a first step.

Appendix

UDL Progression Rubric

Based on the CAST UDL Guidelines (2018)

UDL Progression Rubric

Katie Novak & Kristan Rodriguez

Provide multiple means of
Engagement

		Emerging	Proficient	Progressing Toward Expert Practice
Provide options for recruiting interest (7)	Optimize individual choice and autonomy (7.1)	Offer choices in what students learn (e.g., "choose a country to study" rather than "study France"), how students learn (e.g., use books, videos, and/or teacher instruction to build understanding), and how they express what they know (e.g., "you can create poster or write paragraph").	Encourage students to choose from multiple options to determine what they learn (guided by standards), how they learn, and how they express what they know. Encourage students to suggest additional options if they can still meet the standard.	Empower students to make choices or suggest alternatives for what they will learn, how they will learn, and how they will express what they know in authentic ways. Free them to self-monitor and reflect on their choices with teacher facilitation and feedback but not explicit direction.
	Optimize relevance, value, and authenticity (7.2)	Offer options that highlight what your learners deem relevant, valuable, and meaningful. For example, you may conduct a student survey and then make instructional decisions based on areas of interest.	Encourage students to share what is relevant, valuable and authentic to them and encourage them to suggest teaching and assessment options that would allow them to meet a defined standard, tying in their interests, culture, and personal strengths. This may be done in a weekly exit ticket, or class discussion, for example.	Empower students to make connections between the content, their own interests, and then push them to link their understanding to authentic real-world scenarios and authentic assessments so they can design their own learning experiences with coaching from the teacher. For example, instead of assigning a lab or giving students the choice of two labs, empower them to design their own lab based on the standard and their scientific interests.
	Minimize threats and distractions (7.3)	Offer options that reduce threats and negative distractions for everyone to create a safe space in which learning can occur. For example, have choices for seating, collaborative work, and clear PBIS expectations.	Collaborate with students to define classroom norms and PBIS expectations and encourage students to help to design the classroom so there are multiple options for seating, collaboration, etc..	Empower students to self-advocate and collaborate to identify threats and distractions and then create creative solutions that will allow them to excel. Student voice drives the environment.

CAST | **Until learning has no limits**™

Provide multiple means of
Engagement

		Emerging	Proficient	Progressing Toward Expert Practice
Provide options for sustaining effort and persistence (8)	Heighten salience of goals and objectives (8.1)	Build in "reminders" of both goals and their value. For example, write standards on the board and/or at the top of assessments and projects.	Encourage students to collaboratively discuss goals in light of students' own passions and interests and to choose from various options to reach the goals.	When given the learning standard, have students create personal goals for how they will learn the content, express the content, and challenge themselves throughout the process.
	Vary demands and resources to optimize challenge (8.2)	Provide options for students to learn content with clear degrees of difficulty. For example, "Explore one of the following resources to learn about the Civil War..." and there may be a rigorous primary source document and a video.	Provide multiple options for students to learn content with clear degrees of difficulty which will require them to reflect on the standard and their own strategy for learning. For example, "Choose two of the following six resources to learn about the Civil War..." and there may be rigorous primary source documents, summary documents, videos, and/ or a podcasts from a professor.	Empower students to select their own content and/or own assessments, based on standards, and encourage them to collaborate to add to the multiple options offered to challenge themselves and identify appropriate resources that connect to their interests and passions.
	Foster collaboration and community (8.3)	Provide opportunities for students to learn how to work effectively with others. For example, create cooperative learning groups with clear goals, roles, and responsibilities.	Develop a classroom that values collaborative groupwork. Students construct their own groups and create their own group norms, responsibilities, etc. and students often seek out and work with diverse partners.	Create a classroom culture where students work together to define goals, create strategies, provide feedback to each other and push each other with mastery-oriented feedback while building integrative thinking.
	Increase mastery-oriented feedback (8.4)	Provide feedback that guides learners toward mastery rather than a fixed notion of performance or compliance. For example, provide feedback that encourages the use of specific supports and strategies in the face of challenge.	In addition to providing emerging feedback, empower students to provide mastery-oriented feedback to each other to support specific improvement and increased effort and persistence.	Implement proficient practice and also empower students to use mastery-oriented feedback independently to self-reflect, self-direct, and pursue personal growth in areas of challenge.

UDL Progression Rubric | Page 2
Novak & Rodríguez | ©2018

CAST | Until learning has no limits™

Provide multiple means of **Engagement**		Emerging	Proficient	Progressing Toward Expert Practice
Provide options for self-regulation (9)	Promote expectations and beliefs that optimize motivation (9.1)	Teach students about the power of perseverance and use language and feedback that will allow all students to see themselves as capable learners.	Foster conversations with students to develop relationships and make authentic connections and use their personal passions and interests to help inspire them and push them toward success.	Create a classroom culture where students are empowered and able to support their own self-talk and support one another's positive attitudes toward learning.
	Facilitate personal coping skills and strategies (9.2)	Offer reminders, models, and tools, to assist learners in managing and directing their emotional responses. For example, use stories or simulations to demonstrate coping skills. Offer options for stress release such as alternate seating, fidget tools, mindfulness breaks, etc.	Empower students to deal with difficult challenges by allowing them to choose from multiple strategies to regulate their learning (e.g., a relaxation corner, put on headphones, take a walk).	Encourage students to self-reflect, accurately interpret their feelings, and use appropriate coping strategies and skills to foster learning for themselves and their classmates.
	Develop self-assessment and reflection (9.3)	Provide students with tools so they are reflecting on their learning through rubrics, self-assessment, etc.	Offer multiple models and scaffolds of different self-assessment techniques so students can identify and choose ones that are optimal. For example, these might include ways to collect, measure, and display data from their own behavior and academic performance for the purpose of monitoring growth.	Create a culture where students consistently reflect on the learning process and assessments so they become self-directed learners who grow over time.

CAST | **Until learning has no limits**™

Provide multiple means of
Representation

		Emerging	Proficient	Progressing Toward Expert Practice
Provide options for perception (1)	Offer ways of customizing the display of information (1.1)	Create resources and materials that address variability and meet the needs of more students (e.g., large size print, additional white space, visuals).	Create resources and materials that students can access electronically. Allow students to use their devices to interact with textual, visual and audio information so they can personalize, take notes, increase/decrease size/volume, etc.	Empower students to choose resources and materials that best meet their needs (e.g., watch a video OR explore a handout) so they can personalize their learning themselves without explicit direction from a teacher.
	Offer alternatives for auditory information (1.2)	Provide an embedded option for any information presented aurally. For example, use closed-captions when playing a video.	Provide multiple options for students to choose alternatives to learn content so they don't have to rely on auditory information (e.g., closed captions for video or the choice of reading a text).	Empower students to select auditory alternatives as well as provide them with a framework to locate additional, reputable resources to build their understanding (e.g., resources on how to determine if a website or author is credible).
	Offer alternatives for visual information (1.3)	Provide an embedded option for students so they don't have to rely on visual information. For example, reading aloud to the class while they read along.	Provide multiple options for students to choose alternatives to learn content so they don't have to rely on visual information (e.g., listen to audiobook instead of reading or choose to work with teacher for short pre-sentation).	Empower students to select alternatives to visual information as well as provide them with a framework to locate additional, reputable resources to build their un-derstanding (e.g., resources on how to determine if a website or author is credible).

CAST | Until learning has no limits™

Provide multiple means of

Representation

		Emerging	Proficient	Progressing Toward Expert Practice
Provide options for language, mathematical expressions, and symbols (2)	Clarify vocabulary and symbols (2.1)	Translate idioms, archaic expressions, culturally exclusive phrases, and slang. For example, explicitly teach vocabulary to students using definitions, visuals, explanations, and examples.	In addition to emerging practice, provide students with explicit instruction in context clues so they can independently learn words unfamiliar to them.	Empower students to use available resources to work collaboratively to determine authentic ways to use relevant vocabulary.
	Clarify syntax and structure (2.2)	Clarify unfamiliar syntax (in language or in math formulas) or underlying structure (in diagrams, graphs, illustrations, extended expositions or narratives). For example, highlight the transition words in an essay.	Provide students with resources that will allow they themselves to clarify syntax and structure (such as dictionaries, math reference sheets, thesaurus, etc.)	Empower students to preview material under study, highlight areas in need of clarification, and choose appropriate resources to build knowledge and understanding.
	Support decoding of text, mathematical notation, and symbols (2.3)	Provide direct instruction, prompts, and scaffolded materials for students who struggle to comprehend information. Or provide alternatives, such as visuals, to support this understanding.	Provide strategies and materials (e.g., math reference sheets, context clue strategies, and so forth) that lower barriers to understand and help students figure out notations, symbols, or problems.	Empower students to independently utilize learned strategies to decode text, mathematical notation, and symbols.
	Promote understanding across languages (2.4)	Provide alternative presentations of material, especially for key information or vocabulary. For example, make key information in the dominant language (e.g., English) also available in the first languages of learners with limited-English proficiency. Also, use images AND words, show opposites, etc.	Provide students with access to tools such as apps, websites, and dictionaries to translate material under study and to collaboratively build understanding.	Empower students to independently utilize options to translate material under study, collaborate to build understanding using tools, apps, etc.
	Illustrate through multiple media (2.5)	Present key concepts in one form of symbolic representation (e.g., an expository text or a math equation) with an alternative form (e.g., an illustration, diagram, video, etc.)	Present students with multiple options and symbolic representations to make meaning and allow them to choose options to build comprehension.	Empower students to choose effective resources from multiple options with multiple representations so not all students are required to learn from the same resources.

CAST | Until learning has no limits™

Provide multiple means of

Representation

		Emerging	Proficient	Progressing Toward Expert Practice
Provide options for comprehension (3)	Activate or supply background knowledge (3.1)	Provide all students with background information on content using direct instruction with options for visuals, audio, etc.	Provide students with options that supply or activate relevant prior knowledge, or link to the prerequisite information elsewhere. For example, use advanced organizers (e.g., KWL methods, concept maps) and then encourage students to select resources that will allow them to build appropriate background knowledge.	Empower students to determine gaps in their own background knowledge and then select appropriate resources to build that knowledge in order to achieve the goals of a lesson. For example, begin with a diagnostic assessment and ask students to reflect and create a strategy for filling in gaps in learning.
	Highlight patterns, critical features, big ideas, and relationships (3.2)	Provide explicit cues or prompts to help students recognize the most important features in information. For example, teach students to use outlines, graphic organizers, highlighters, etc.	Provide students with options and multiple strategies to support recognition of the most important features in information. For example, allow them to use outlines, graphic organizer, highlighter, word cloud apps, and other organizing tools.	Empower students to self-reflect to determine the most effective strategies for highlighting critical information and independently select the strategies that allow them to support recognition of patterns, critical features, big ideas, and relationships.
	Guide information processing, visualization, and manipulation (3.3)	Provide all students with materials, strategies, and tools to support processing and visualization. Tools include manipulatives (i.e, counting cubes), glossaries, graphic organizers, and more.	Provide students with options of multiple materials, strategies, and tools to use to support processing and visualization, such as the option to make visual notes, use technology to locate images, and/or select and use manipulatives, etc.	Empower students to self-reflect and independently choose the most appropriate materials, strategies, and tools to guide information processing, visualization, and manipulation, searching for additional tools and strategies, if necessary.
	Maximize transfer and generalization (3.4)	Model explicit strategies students can use to transfer the information they have to other content areas and situations. For example, show how the knowledge could be used in another class or be used to make comparisons across content in the class (such as text to text comparisons).	Provide options for meaningful transfer, such as interdisciplinary projects, where students can make authentic connections and apply knowledge in meaningful ways in other content areas and in authentic situations.	Encourage students to apply knowledge and skills learned in class to enhance their understanding of content, design of their own authentic projects, and express their knowledge and understanding in authentic, real-world scenarios.

CAST | **Until learning has no limits**™

Provide multiple means of **Action & Expression**		Emerging	Proficient	Progressing Toward Expert Practice
Provide options for physical action (4)	Vary the methods for response and navigation (4.1)	Provide more than one option for the methods used for response and navigation within the same assignment. For example, some students may use IPads while others write by hand.	Provide multiple options for the methods used for response and navigation within the same assignment. For example, some students may use IPads, different writing utensils, keyboards, voice recognition software, etc.	Empower students to use their own devices to respond to and interact with materials for all assignments (e.g., options to use headphones, keyboards, manipulatives, joysticks, etc.).
	Optimize access to tools and assistive technologies (4.2)	Allow some students to use assistive technologies for navigation, interaction, and composition if required by an IEP or 504.	Provide multiple options for all students to use assistive technology like IPads, voice recognition, and 1:1 devices regardless of variability.	Empower students to assess the need for and choose technologies that work for them to provide additional, personalized options to express their knowledge and skills.
Provide options for expression and communication (5)	Use multiple media for communication (5.1)	Provide more than one way to answer on assessments so students can express their understanding without barriers. Taking a traditional test may be one option, but so, too, could be an oral presentation or writing an essay.	Provide students with multiple options to express their understanding—and let them suggest some ways of being assessed, so they understand that showing what they know is the point rather than how well they perform on a particular kind of test. Students may choose to express their understanding in text, audio, video, multimedia, live presentations, and many other ways.	Let students reflect on a standard or a set of competency or proficiency-based rubrics, and then independently create authentic and innovative products that allow them to demonstrate their mastery of the standard.
	Use multiple tools for construction and composition (5.2)	Provide the choice of more than one tool or strategy to help students express their knowledge. For example, allow students to compose a response using traditional pen and paper or allow them to create a multimedia presentation on their device.	Provide multiple tools and strategies to help students express their knowledge. For example, allow students to compose a response using traditional written methods, blogging software, or multimedia tools such as ThingLink or Emaze.	When provided with a task, or when independently creating an authentic product, students are empowered to self-reflect and select tools and materials that will support their learning and challenge them to strive for rigorous options to express knowledge and skills in accessible, engaging ways using, and then building upon, the tools they were exposed to in class.
	Build fluencies with graduated levels of support for practice and performance (5.3)	Implement a scaffolding model from teacher-directed to collaborative groups to independent work, slowly releasing responsibility to students. For example, in collaborative work, assign team members specific tasks and monitor their progress before moving to independent work or move from teacher-directed instruction to Socratic seminars.	Provide options for support and scaffolding throughout the learning process and encourage students to choose resources that allow them to build their own knowledge while working in collaborative groups and working independently. In collaborative groups, for example, encourage students to self-select roles; in class discussions, have students collaborate to design the rules and structures.	Empower students to create challenges that let them productively struggle to reach rigorous goals and use supports as tools to help them to make improvements rather than making things "easier." Encourage students to provide feedback and drive teacher instruction; encourage them to define roles and expectations for group work that include routine monitoring and reflection.

CAST | Until learning has no limits™

Provide multiple means of
Action & Expression

		Emerging	Proficient	Progressing Toward Expert Practice
Provide options for executive functions (6)	Guide appropriate goal-setting (6.1)	Provide clear goals to students so it's clear what they must do to meet or exceed expectations. For example, post standards on the board and on assignments, and articulate those standards and goals throughout the lesson.	Create conditions for learners to develop goal-setting skills. For example, provide students with standards on the board and on assignments, but also provide models or examples of the process and product of goal setting so all students can develop personalized goals while working toward standards.	Encourage students to create personalized learning plans that include goals that align to identified standards as well as action plans and strategies that optimize personal strengths while addressing individualized areas of challenge.
	Support planning and strategy development (6.2)	Facilitate the process of strategic planning. For example, provide all students with checklists for tasks, due dates, and planning templates to keep students organized.	Facilitate the process of strategic planning. For example, provide students not only with organizational tools but with scaffolds they need to create personalized strategies to meet their goals.	Empower students to self-reflect, self-assess, and create personalized action plans to achieve their identified goals. For example, encourage students to reflect on how much time and resources they need to perform selected tasks and then encourage them to make personal due dates and task lists to reach their goals.
	Facilitate managing information and resources (6.3)	Provide scaffolds and supports to act as organizational aids for students. For example, provide all students with templates for note-taking.	Provide exposure to multiple scaffolds, supports, and resources that act as organization aids, such as a variety of graphic organizers or different strategies for note-taking.	Empower students to self-reflect, self-assess, and independently choose the most appropriate supports and resources that will allow them to organize information and resources so they can achieve their identified goal(s).
	Enhance capacity for monitoring progress (6.4)	Provide formative feedback tools to students so they can monitor their own progress. For example, provide students with assessment checklists, scoring rubrics, and multiple examples of annotated student work/performance examples.	Provide multiple opportunities for students to receive feedback from the teacher, peers, and themselves using a variety of tools such as assessment checklists, scoring rubrics, and exemplars.	Empower students to use multiple resources, including teachers and peers, to consistently reflect on their performance, collect feedback, and revise their work to promote and highlight growth.

CAST | Until learning has no limits™

References

Anderson, L. H. (2011). *Speak*. New York: Square Fish.

Arnaiz Sánchez, P., de Haro Rodríguez, R., & Maldonado Martínez, R. M. (2019). Barriers to student learning and participation in an inclusive school as perceived by future education professionals. *Journal of New Approaches in Educational Research, 8*(1), 18–24.

Brewer, D. J., Rees, D. I., & Argys, L. (1995). Detracking America's schools: The reform without cost? *Phi Delta Kappan, 77*, 210–212.

Brown, B. (2018, October 5). It's not fear that gets in the way of daring leadership. It's our armor. Retrieved from https://www.linkedin.com/pulse/why-vulnerability-essential-becoming-great-leader-bren%C3%A9-brown/

Bumen, N. T., Cakar, E., & Yildiz, D. G. (2014). Curriculum fidelity and factors affecting fidelity in the Turkish context. *Educational Sciences: Theory and Practice, 14*(1), 219–228.

Canaday, S. (2012, October 8). How to detect your blind spots that make your colleagues disrespect you. *Forbes*. Retrieved from https://www.forbes.com/sites/forbesleadershipforum/2012/10/08/how-to-detect-your-blind-spots-that-make-your-colleagues-disrespect-you/?sh=69a0b540576e

CAST. (2018). *UDL Guidelines*. Wakefield, MA. Retrieved from https://udlguidelines.cast.org

Center for Teaching Quality. (2013). Measuring learning, supporting teaching: Classroom experts' recommendations for an effective educator evaluation system. Center for Teaching Quality. Retrieved from https://eric.ed.gov/?id=ED544418

Coelho, P. (1998). *The alchemist.* San Francisco: HarperSanFrancisco.

Commission on Teacher Credentialing. (2009). California standards for the teaching profession (CSTP). Retrieved from https://www.cde .ca.gov/pd/ps/

Cook, S. C., & Rao, K. (2018). Systematically applying UDL to effective practices for students with learning disabilities. *Learning Disability Quarterly, 41*(3), 179–191.

Council of the Great City Schools. (2017). *Supporting excellence: A framework for developing, implementing, and sustaining a high-quality district curriculum. First edition.* Council of the Great City Schools.

Danielson Group, The. (2020). *Our story.* Retrieved from https:// danielsongroup.org/our-story

Delisle, J. R. (1999, November). For gifted students, full inclusion is a partial solution. *Educational Leadership, 57*(3), 80–83.

Diedrich, J., Neubauer, A. C., & Ortner, A. (2018). The prediction of professional success in apprenticeship: The role of cognitive and noncognitive abilities, of interests and personality. *International Journal for Research in Vocational Education and Training, 5*(2), 82–111.

Doig, B., & Groves, S. (2011). Japanese lesson study: Teacher professional development through communities of inquiry. *Mathematics Teacher Education and Development, 13*(1), 77–93.

DuFour, R., DuFour, R., Eaker, R., & Many, T. (2010). *Learning by doing: A handbook for professional learning communities at work.* Bloomington, IN: Solution Tree Press.

Dweck, C. S. (2006). *Mindset: The new psychology of success.* New York: Random House.

ERS. (2018). *Finding time for collaborative planning.* Retrieved from https://www.erstrategies.org/cms/files/3876-finding-time-for -collaborative-planning.pdf

Eurich, T. (2018, January 4). What self-awareness really is (and how to cultivate it). *Harvard Business Review.* Retrieved from https://hbr .org/2018/01/what-self-awareness-really-is-and-how-to-cultivate-it

Ganias, M., & Novak, K. (2020). Universally designing your faculty meetings and PLCs in the virtual world. Retrieved from https://www .novakeducation.com/wp-content/uploads/2020/04/Video _Conferencing_PLC_Guide_REV.pdf

Gladwell, M. (2000). *The tipping point: How little things can make a big difference.* New York: Little, Brown and Company.

Goleman, D., Boyatzis, R. E., & McKee, A. (2013). *Primal leadership: Realizing the power of emotional intelligence.* Cambridge, MA: Harvard Business School Press.

Haslam, R. E. (2018). Checking our bias at the door: Centering our core values in the classroom. *Literacy Today, 36*(1), 24–26.

Hehir, T., Grindal, T., & Eidelman, H. (2012). Review of special education in the commonwealth of Massachusetts. Massachusetts Department of Elementary and Secondary Education. Retrieved from http://www.doe.mass.edu/sped/hehir/

Heifetz, R. A., & Linsky, M. (2002). *Leadership on the line: Staying alive through the dangers of leading.* Boston, MA: Harvard Business School Press.

Iizuka, C. A., Barrett, P. M., Gillies, R., Cook, C. R., & Marinovic, W. (2015). Preliminary evaluation of the FRIENDS for Life program on students' and teachers' emotional states for a school in a low socio-economic status area. *Australian Journal of Teacher Education, 40*(3). Retrieved from https://ro.ecu.edu.au/ajte/vol40/iss3/1/

Kivunja, C. (2018). Distinguishing between theory, theoretical framework, and conceptual framework: A systematic review of lessons from the field. *International Journal of Higher Education, 7*(6), 44–53. Retrieved from https://eric.ed.gov/?id=EJ1198682

Larsen, D. E., & Hunter, J. E. (2014, October). Separating wheat from chaff: How secondary school principals' core values and beliefs influence decision-making related to mandates. *International Journal of Educational Leadership Preparation, 9*(2), 71–90.

Lavigne, H. J., Shakman, K., Zweig, J., & Greller, S. L. (2016). Principals' time, tasks, and professional development: An analysis of Schools and Staffing Survey data (REL 2017–201). Washington, DC: U.S. Department of Education, Institute of Education Sciences, National Center for Education Evaluation and Regional Assistance, Regional Educational Laboratory Northeast & Islands. Retrieved from https://eric.ed.gov/?id=ED569168

Lewin, K (1947). Frontiers in group dynamics: Concept, method and reality in social science; equilibrium and social change. *Human Relations 1*(1): 5–41.

Massachusetts Department of Elementary and Secondary Education. (2016). Advice from teachers and administrators: Using student & staff feedback to improve practice. Malden, MA. Retrieved from https://www.doe.mass.edu/edeval/evidence/feedback/improve-practice.docx

Massachusetts Department of Elementary and Secondary Education. (2019). Multi-tiered system of support: Blueprint for MA. Malden, MA. Retrieved from https://matoolsforschools.com/resources/mtss-blueprint

McChesney, C., Covey, S., & Huling, J. (2012). *The 4 disciplines of execution: Achieving your wildly important goals.* New York, NY: Free Press.

Meo, G. (2008). Curriculum planning for all learners: Applying universal design for learning (UDL) to a high school reading comprehension program. *Preventing School Failure, 52*(2), 21–30. Retrieved from https://www.tandfonline.com/doi/abs/10.3200/PSFL.52.2.21-30

Meyer, A., Rose, D. H., & Gordon, D. (2014). *Universal design for learning: Theory and practice.* Wakefield, MA: CAST Professional Publishing.

Murata, A., & Kim-Eng Lee, C. (2020). *Stepping up lesson study: An educator's guide to deeper learning.* London: Routledge.

National Council on Disabilities (2018). *IDEA Series: The segregation of students with disabilities.* Retrieved from https://ncd.gov/sites/default/files/NCD_Segregation-SWD_508.pdf

National Council of Learning Disabilities & Understood. (2019). *Forward together: A school leader's guide to building inclusive schools.* Retrieved from https://www.ncld.org/wp-content/uploads/2019/12/Guide-to-Creating-Inclusive-Schools-12.9.2019.pdf

Novak, K., & Rodriguez, K. (2018). UDL progression rubric. Retrieved from http://castpublishing.org/novak-rodriguez-udl-progression-rubric/

Novak, K., & Rodriguez, K. (2016). *Universally designed leadership: Applying UDL to systems and schools.* Wakefield, MA: CAST.

Olofson, M. W., Downes, J. M., Petrick Smith, C., LeGeros, L., & Bishop, P. A. (2018). An instrument to measure teacher practices to support personalized learning in the middle grades. *Research in Middle Level Education Online, 41*(7), 1–21.

Posey, A., & Novak, K. (2020). *Unlearning: Changing your beliefs and classroom with UDL.* Wakefield, MA: CAST Professional Publishing.

Potter, H. (2019). Integrating classrooms and reducing academic tracking strategies for school leaders and educators. The Century

Foundation. Retrieved from https://tcf.org/content/report/integrating
-classrooms-reducing-academic-tracking-strategies-school-leaders
-educators/

Pulakos, E. D., & Schmitt, N. (1995). Experience-based and situational interview questions: Studies of validity. *Personnel Psychology, 48*(2), 289–308. Retrieved from https://doi.org/10.1111/j.1744-6570.1995 .tb01758.x

Reardon, R., Fite, K., Boone, M., & Sullivan, S. (2019). Critically reflective leadership: Defining successful growth. *International Journal of the Whole Child, 4*(1), 20–32. Retrieved from https://eric.ed.gov /?q=fite+boone&id=EJ1213738

Redding, S., Corbett, J., & Center on School Turnaround at WestEd. (2018). Shifting school culture to spark rapid improvement: A quick start guide for principals and their teams. *The Center on School Turnaround Four Domains Series.* Retrieved from https://csti.wested .org/resource/shifting-school-culture-to-spark-rapid-improvement -a-quick-start-guide-for-principals-and-their-teams/

Rose, D. H., & Meyer, A. (2002). *Teaching every student in the digital age: Universal Design for Learning.* Alexandria, VA: ASCD.

Rose, T. (2016). *The end of average: How we succeed in a world that values sameness.* San Francisco, CA: Harper Collins.

Rothman, R., & Jobs for the Future. (2018, July). Measuring deeper learning: New directions in formative assessment. *Students at the Center: Deeper Learning Research Series.* Jobs for the Future. https:// www.jff.org/resources/measuring-deeper-learning/

Saunders, M., de Velasco, J. R., & Oakes, J. (2017). *Learning time: In pursuit of educational equity.* Harvard Education Press.

Schein, E. H. (1999). Kurt Lewin's change theory in the field and in the classroom: Notes toward a model of managed learning. *Reflections, 1*(1), 59–74.

Schlechty, P. (2011). *Engaging students: The next level of working on the work.* San Francisco, CA: Jossey-Bass.

Scott, L. A. (2018). Barriers with implementing a universal design for learning framework. *Inclusion, 6*(4), 274–286.

Smith, K. G., Dombek, J. L., Foorman, B. R., Hook, K. S., Lee, L., Cote, A.-M. (2016). Self-study guide for implementing high school academic interventions. (REL 2016-218.) Tallahassee, FL: Regional Educational Laboratory Southeast.

Stone, D., & Heen, S. (2015). *Thanks for the feedback.* Portfolio Penguin.

Venning, J., & Buisman-Pijlman, F. (2013). Integrating assessment matrices in feedback loops to promote research skill development in postgraduate research projects. *Assessment & Evaluation in Higher Education, 38*(5), 567–579.

Acknowledgments

From Katie

I am a big fan of Ed Sheeran, and especially his *No.6 Collaborations Album.* I imagine him growing as an artist with each person he produces music with: Justin Bieber, Khalid, Chris Stapleton and Bruno Mars, and Camilla Cabello and Cardi B, among others. I too count myself blessed that I have had so many opportunities to collaborate with brilliant artists. This book is my eighth collaboration. I have co-written books with Tom Thibodeau (my daddy!), Kristan Rodriguez, Sean Bracken, Allison Posey, George Couros, Mirko Chardin, and Catlin Tucker. This book, my *No. 8 Collaboration Album,* is with my dear friend, Mike Woodlock.

Mike, it has been a pleasure to work with you and write with you. I learned so much from you as a leader, not the least of which was the "Good Cop" routine and your incredible use of, "Oh, you think this is funny?" You are a genius at fostering courageous conversations, and I channel you when I have to have those conversations myself. I owe you a lifetime of Lays potato chips for everything you have taught me. And send my love to Keliann, who had to deal with our nighttime and weekend writing routine for two years. Maybe I should send the chips to her! And if you're wondering who you are in the Ed Sheeran album, you're obviously Bieber.

To David Gordon. For being my long-lost Pawtucket brother and an amazing editor, publisher, and friend. You believed in my writing first, and I can't thank you enough for helping me become the writer and educator I am today. I heard "No," so many times before you. But you said "Yes," and that made all the difference. Thank you for your faith in me. Cheers to Book #10.

To my husband, Lon Novak, and his assistant, Don Kovack, thank you for all the laughs. And to my babies—Torin, Aylin, Brecan, and Boden. This is all for you.

From Mike

I honestly never imagined I would write a book. But, if someone believes you are capable of something, you may actually start believing them. With that in mind I want to thank my co-author who shocked me a while back when she told me that we should write a book together. I am so honored to have co-written this book with my talented and amazing friend, Katie Novak. I am lucky to have such a positive influence in my professional and personal life. I learn and laugh whenever we are together. What a wonderful combination!

To John Morse, my former teacher, later a colleague, and always a friend who saw an educator in me before I ever saw one in myself. I am not sure you realize how much of an impact you had on me. I am glad to have this opportunity to let you know how much I appreciate the opportunity you gave me.

Thank you to my wonderful colleagues at Groton-Dunstable Regional High School, Tyngsborough High School, and Chaminade-Madonna College Preparatory as well as all my friends and mentors along the way who have provided me with the experience necessary to co-author this book.

To my Mom and Dad who gave me everything and sacrificed so much so that I could pursue my dreams. To Steven, Richard, and Laurie who have always been there for me. And to my family I married into: thank you for always loving me as your own. I love you all.

Acknowledgments

To Keliann, thanks for the support and modeling what an educator should be. To Anna, Thomas, and Katy, thanks for making me laugh, making me proud, and keeping me humble. To quote Katy, "I love the five of us."

About the Authors

Katie Novak, EdD, is an internationally renowned education consultant, a graduate instructor at the University of Pennsylvania, Graduate School of Education, and author of nine books on inclusive practices, including bestselling *UDL Now!, Innovate Inside the Box* with George Couros, and *Equity by Design* with Mirko Chardin.

Novak has provided in-person professional development, long-term implementation, and consulting in Universal Design for Learning (UDL), inclusive practices, and equity in education in 27 states and 10 countries and has worked with high-profile clients such as the NASA Science Activation Team, the Gates Foundation, Harvard University, Los Angeles Unified School District, and PBS Learning Media.

Additionally, Novak has worked directly with state departments of education in Ohio, Washington, Minnesota, Hawaii, Wisconsin, Arizona, California, and Massachusetts to provide professional learning on UDL and the development of research-based multitiered systems of support and has worked with the U.S. Department of Education Jobs for the Future (JFF) through the School Turnaround Learning Community and with the Office of Special Education Programs.

Her work in UDL has been highlighted in many publications including *Edutopia, Language Magazine, ADDitude, Common-Wealth Magazine, The Inclusion Lab, Think Inclusive, eSchool*

News, HuffPost, District Administrator, ASCD Education Update, and *School Administrator.*

Mike Woodlock is an innovative administrator, consultant, and graduate instructor who embraces change. As an acting principal in Massachusetts with 25 years of experience in education, Woodlock has the unique experience of being hired as a high school principal in a district where he was immediately tasked with implementing a strategic plan that required a complete transformation of the education system through the lens of UDL.

Having experienced the barriers that come with the implementation of UDL, he offers concrete insights about how to increase staff engagement, transition staffing and schedules, and implement innovative pilot programs by creating conditions of nurture for all staff while also improving school culture and community. Woodlock has worked with administrators across the country, supporting the implementation of multitiered systems of support, inclusive practice, and UDL.

As a graduate instructor, Woodlock has been working with the Washington Association of School Administrators (WASA) as a part of the statewide Inclusive Practice Project (IPP), a project that helped to significantly improve the state's inclusion rates. His work with UDL was highlighted in a publication by the National Association of Secondary School Principals, *Principal Leadership.*

Index

professional learning
  designing, 67
  faculty meetings, 57–59
  instructional rounds, 55–57
  power of, 48
  providing, 83–84
professional practice, domains of, 63
Pulakos, E. D., & Schmitt, N., 99

Q
questions. *See* self-reflection questions

R
Reardon, R., Fite, K., Boone, M., and
  Sullivan, S., 8
Redding, S., Corbett, J., & Center on
  School Turnaround at WestEd, 40
reflecting on strengths and
  weaknesses, 15–17
relationship management and
  jaggedness, 11
remote learning, preparing for, 12–13.
  See also learning
representation
  providing means of, 36
  UDL Progression Rubric, 138–140
research projects, conducting, 91–92
review committee, establishing for
  curriculum, 85–86
risks, taking, 19–20, 129, 132–133
Rodriguez, Kristan, 45
Rose, Todd, 9, 11
Rose, D. H., & Meyer, A., 35
Rothman & Jobs for the Future, 84
rubrics
  collaboration and community,
    71–72
  curriculum adoption, 88–89
  teacher evaluation, 62, 68
  UDL Progression, 135–142

S
Saunders, M., de Valasco, J. R., &
  Oakes, J., 2017, 113
schedules. *See also* planning time
  activities, 113

with additional time, 117
addressing barriers to, 126
adoption tips, 118
defining sufficient time, 113
elementary considerations, 119
enrichment opportunities, 114–115
impact of COVID on, 114
making whole-scale changes, 125
middle schools, 122
open honors high school pilot,
  123–126
reflection questions, 112
secondary considerations,
  120–123
student interests and needs, 114
technical barriers, 112
Tier 2 and Tier 3 instruction, 115
UDL-informed, 115
universal design, 114
working with teachers, 117
Schein, Edgar Henry, 3
Schlechty, P., 35
school leaders, as expert learners, 6.
  See also leaders
Scott, L. A., 34
secondary schedule considerations,
  120–123
self-assessment, fostering, 15–17
self-awareness
  and jaggedness, 10
  lack of, 15
self-confidence and jaggedness, 10
self-differentiated learning, 83
self-management and jaggedness, 10
self-perception, weakness of, 15
self-reflection questions
  curriculum, 96
  educator evaluations, 76
  executive function, 30
  expert learners, 6–7, 20
  professional learning, 59
  schedules, 127
  staffing, 109
  UDL foundation, 46
service and jaggedness, 11
skills in KSBCs, 100–102

ALSO BY **Katie Novak**
from CAST Professional Publishing

UDL Now! A Teacher's Guide to Applying Universal Design for Learning in Today's Classrooms

By Katie Novak, with a foreword by David H. Rose, Co-Founder of CAST

ISBN 978-1-930583-66-5 (Paper)
240 pages · 6 x 9 · US $34.99
Available in print and accessible e-book formats.

In this **revised and expanded** edition of the bestseller *UDL Now!* Katie Novak provides **practical insights** and **savvy strategies** for helping all learners meet high standards using the principles of Universal Design for Learning (UDL).

Novak shows how to use the UDL Guidelines to **plan lessons, choose materials, assess learning,** and **improve instructional practice**. She discusses key concepts such as **scaffolding, vocabulary-building,** and **using student feedback** to inform instruction. She also provides tips on recruiting students as partners in the teaching process, engaging their interest in how they learn.

This revised version includes new chapters on **differentiated instruction** as well as how to engage students more effectively. Also, each chapter includes helpful discussion questions to facilitate group study.

UDL Now! is a fun and effective Monday-morning playbook for great teaching.

To order, visit www.castpublishing.org or wherever books are sold

Universally Designed Leadership— Applying UDL to Systems and Schools

By Katie Novak and Kristan Rodriguez

Katie Novak
Kristan Rodriguez

UNIVERSALLY DESIGNED LEADERSHIP
Applying UDL to Systems and Schools

"*Universally Designed Leadership* is the practitioners' guide to successful strategic implementation of Universal Design for Learning. This timely and relevant work provides a road map for education leaders to engage school communities in defining the why, what, and how of learning. A must read for emerging and veteran school leaders alike."

—Dr. Thomas Scott, Executive Director of the Massachusetts Association of School Superintendents

ISBN 978-1930583-6-27 (Paperback)
ISBN 978-1930583-6-34 (ePUB)
136 pages · 6 x 9 · US $34.99
Available in print and accessible e-book formats.

U.S. education policy and that of many states defines and endorses Universal Design for Learning (UDL) as a framework to help achieve **greater opportunity** and academic achievement for all learners and at **all grade levels**, from preK to postsecondary to workforce training.

In this book, Novak and Rodriguez, veteran school administrators, provide school leaders with a practical handbook for putting UDL to work in their schools and districts. They show how to guide staff in discussions around student data and use the UDL Guidelines to **shape curriculum decisions**. This is a **must-read** for any education leader who wants to create more equitable, inclusive, and effective learning environments.

To order, visit www.castpublishing.org or wherever books are sold

CPSIA information can be obtained
at www.ICGtesting.com
Printed in the USA
LVHW082250060522
718085LV00036B/1073